One Step At A Time

My Journey To Everest Base Camp

Paul Tallett

Copyright © 2020 by Paul Tallett

All rights reserved

No part of this publication may be reproduced, stored in or introduced into a retrieval system or transmitted by any other form or by any means without the prior written consent of the author.

Also, this book may not be hired out whether for a fee or otherwise in any cover other than supplied by the author

ISBN: 9798695554861

Published by www.publishandprint.co.uk

**For my wonderful wife Caroline,
with her support anything is possible!**

CONTENTS

Introduction	7
Part One – A Mountain To Climb	9
Couch to 3k (feet)	9
Dodging a bullet and discovering Everest	14
How to admit defeat on the mountains	18
Running on empty	21
Part Two – My Journey To Base Camp	24
Kathmandu – Rammechap – Surkey	28
Surkey – Phakding – Namche	38
Acclimatisation Day at Namche	50
Namche – Phortse	59
Phortse – Dingboche	67
Dingboche – Lobouche	79
Lobuche – Gorak Shep – Everest Base Camp – Gorak Shep	84

Gorak Shep – Pangboche	104
Pangboche – Namche	107
Namche – Lukla	114
Lukla – Kathmandu	121
Sacred Memories	131
Leaving Nepal	142
Epilogue	146
Equipment	148
Toiletries And Medication	153
Cost Of Trip	155

INTRODUCTION

I spent my 40th birthday at Everest Base Camp. This book will tell you exactly how I got there, day-by-day, during an unforgettable experience that I hope many of you reading this will be able to share. As I prepared for my own expedition, I read a lot of information about what lay ahead, but nothing I could relate to, as an ordinary person about to embark on the adventure of a lifetime. I hope, as you read my diary, you will be able to imagine your own journey.

For me, that took 10 years. Not all of it is described in detail here, but before I tell you about the days I spent in the Himalayas, let me explain how a 30-year-old who spent weekends stoned on the sofa, accompanied by takeaway pizza, ended up at the front of his group, tears of joy and exhaustion streaming down his face as he reached Base Camp.

Between that sofa and those tears there were literally hundreds of mountains, a couple of near-death experiences, one debilitating illness and too many good times and friendships to list here. But there is certainly room for some of them.

PART ONE – A MOUNTAIN TO CLIMB

Couch to 3k (feet)

My name is Paul Tallett. I grew up in social housing in Cumbernauld, a town approximately 10 miles outside Glasgow, built due to a chronic shortage of housing in that city after World War II. I'm the eldest of three children, along with my sisters Julie and Karen.

My Dad, Peter, worked as a joiner. He worked overtime on Tuesdays and Thursdays and then took a Sunday shift to bring in extra money for his family. Money was tight for us, but we got by because of that and it ingrained in me an understanding of the value of hard work.

Like many kids growing up in Scotland, my sole past-time and interest was football. Myself and my band of friends played most days and during the summer holidays would play from sunrise until sunset or until the street lights came on, which would be our cue to go home for the night.

I played for a football team called Seafar Villa and in 1991 managed to win the award for Player of the Year. My trophy was presented to me by the former Celtic captain and my hero, Roy Aitken. However, that was to be the pinnacle of my football career. Soon after, I left school and started my working life selling contractor's tools, work wear and personal protective equipment (PPE).

I was doing well at work, and the money was good enough to

pay for four or five holidays each year, but I found myself drifting from one weekend to the next, spent smoking cannabis and eating Dominos pizza.

This changed in 2009, when a business acquaintance asked if I wanted to climb Ben Nevis, the highest mountain in the United Kingdom, to raise funds for the hospital where his 18-month-old son tragically passed away after an accident at home.

Looking over to Ben Lui from the top of Ben Dorain.

I asked some friends and colleagues if they wanted to get fit and climb Ben Nevis whilst raising money for a great cause and we were committed and ready to go.

My brother-in-law, Stephen, had some hill walking experience and decided our first training mountain should be

Ben Ledi, a Corbett[1] just outside the picturesque village of Callander. The sun was shining and the views were amazing. We even smoked a joint at the summit and had a pint in a local pub afterwards. This hill walking gig was a piece of piss!

Two weeks later, and now joined by my friends Colin and Thomas, we took on our first Munro: Ben Lomond, standing at 3248 feet, or 990m. We reached halfway under another glorious sun, feeling fine. These mountains were easy.

However, by the time we reached the summit, cloud had reduced visibility to less than four metres and the rain was coming down in buckets. My inexperience was laid bare. No gloves, no waterproofs and we were all getting cold very quickly.

We decided to descend via the lesser-used Ptarmigan route. However, after a few hours the car park was nowhere to be seen and we were, as far as we could tell, still high up the mountain. Panic began to set in.

Once again – and for the last time on the mountains – a joint was produced, and this one appeared to have magical properties. As we passed it around, the cloud cleared and we could see our way down. We were back in the car around an hour later: a little shaken and very wet. I had been bitten by the Munro bug.

[1] The Scottish mountains have classifications. A Corbett is between 2500 and 3000 feet (there are 222 of these in Scotland); a Munro is a mountain over 3000 feet (there are 282 of these).

Me at the top of Ben Lomond.

I trained hard in the weeks that followed, as our charity trek up the tallest mountain in the United Kingdom loomed larger and larger on my calendar. A few weeks before my date with Ben Nevis, my wife and I went on holiday to Croatia. Just before we were due to leave, however, I felt the beginnings of what I thought was a chest infection. My family doctor was on holiday and a locum told me I had an asthma flare-up, and I'd be fine after a week in the sun. However, I struggled with my breathing throughout the holiday and when I returned and saw my usual doctor, I was diagnosed with a serious chest infection. *No shit, Sherlock.*

The group who climbed Ben Nevis for charity. only 1 person never made it to the summit, me!

Over the next few days it got progressively worse, and I made a second appointment to see the doctor. The message was clear: there was no chance of me summiting Ben Nevis without seriously risking my health or even having to be rescued from the mountain.

As the organiser, I decided to make the trip to support our team of nine: Stephen, Colin, Neil, Thomas, Aldo, Scott, Gavin and Stuart. We stayed in a hostel just outside Fort William in the western Highlands, the gateway to Ben Nevis, on the shores of Loch Linnhe. The hostel was not the most salubrious of accommodations, but it met our needs for the two nights we were staying.

My plan was to organise the guys and ensure they got a summit photograph for the charity. I would sit in my car, feeling sorry for myself. However, bravery or stupidity got the better of me. I initially planned to walk the first 20-30 minutes with the guys, before heading back. Before I knew it, I was on the famous zig-zags on the tourist route, a mere 30 minutes from the summit. But I was struggling to breathe and taking hits of my inhaler every ten steps. Common sense prevailed and I turned around, wondering what might have been. The rest of the team made it to the summit and raised a phenomenal amount of money for Edinburgh Sick Kids Hospital.

Dodging a bullet and discovering Everest

I continued to climb hills near to my home throughout the winter of 2009/2010, gaining experience and fitness. This was my hobby now, and I was telling everybody in my life about it. And so a business acquaintance, Scott Walker, who had some hillwalking experience, invited me to climb two Munros: Beinn Ime and Beinn Narnain, from the Butter Bridge route at the Rest and Be Thankful pass in Argyll in the early spring of April 2010. It was a trip from which I would return with a valuable lesson about the mountains, but I was fortunate to return at all.

We made it up Beinn Ime, the highest mountain in the Arrochar range at over 1000m. It was 15 degrees Celsius when we got out of the car, yet we were caught in a snowstorm as we neared the summit. The ridge was covered in leftover winter snow and some fresh stuff.

I walked onto what I know now, but did not know then, to be a cornice: a deceptive accumulation of snow that overhangs a ridge, but looks to the novice to be a part of the mountain itself. In reality, it is just snow, often deposited by a recent drift, underneath which is nothing but air. As I stepped onto this snow my legs disappeared and I was left dangling, with my torso above the snow and my legs underneath the cornice, with a drop to my death underneath that.

Scott pulled me out, and in my ignorance and inexperience I was unaware of the extent of the danger I had been in. Scott wisely decided one Munro was enough and we walked back to the car park in Arrochar.

The more I spoke to people about my new obsession, the more I realised how popular a pastime hillwalking is in Scotland. Aldo, a friend who had been part of that first charity walk up Ben Nevis, and I decided to climb Beinn Ghlas and Ben Lawers, just outside Killin, a village west of Stirling, famous for the Falls of Dochart. I was getting to see places in Scotland I never knew existed when I was spending weekends sitting at home in Airdrie, smoking cannabis and eating pizzas, and I fell in love with Killin. My wife Caroline and I would visit many times and eventually buy a holiday home there, in 2016 – since then we've sold and upgraded to a larger house there. We absolutely love Killin.

Those wasted weekends were a thing of the past, as were the drugs. I have Obsessive Compulsive Disorder (OCD) and the hills were now my focus. After Beinn Ghlas and Ben Lawers, and a successful rematch against my nemesis, Ben Nevis, I barely stopped: I climbed 17 Munros in 2011, 36 in 2012. But it wasn't just the 3000-ft giants that I was interested in; I was out every weekend in the Campsie, Ochill, Pentland and Border hills. I would recruit teammates whenever I could, such as Jim Fowler and Peter Henry, two business acquaintances who became great companions over the years. I met Ricky Reid and Paul Leckie on two Munros at Drumochter and both became great friends. 2013 brought another 33 Munros and Paul and Ricky were pushing my fitness levels: we were taking in four Munros at a time.

In October 2013 Ricky and I headed up to the Fannich range, just outside Ullapool, to climb five Munros. We stayed in a bunkhouse the night before to ensure a good night's sleep before a big day on the hills. When we arrived at the bunkhouse, there was a fellow walker in our room. We exchanged some stories and I invited Phil Galloway to join us the next day, primarily to keep me company as Ricky is super-fast on the hills. That was the beginning of a great friendship. Phil is an amazing, selfless walking companion and friend and would help me through one of the hardest points of my life.

At the top of my 100th Munro in the Fannichs.

Now I was looking further afield: I climbed two mountains in Italy, arriving at 2200 metres above sea level, 855m higher than the UK's tallest peak, Ben Nevis.

Also in 2013, the idea of Mount Everest came into clear focus on the horizon. My wife Caroline joined me on a trip up Conic Hill, near Balmaha. On our descent we met two ladies, Sandra and Zoe, who told me they were planning a trek to Everest Base Camp. By sheer chance we bumped into them again on Ben A'nn, in the Trossachs, a few weeks later and I quizzed them all about their trip.

I had begun to read about Everest at the very start of my journey into the hills: perhaps it was in my nature to instantly explore the tallest peak in the world, albeit remotely. I read about George Mallory's pioneering explorations of the mountain on which he died, in 1924. There is a theory that Mallory and Andrew Irvine were the first to make it to the summit, before perishing on the descent. They were last seen 245 metres from the top. They found Mallory's frozen body in 1999, 75 years after he died; Irvine's body has yet to be found.

The first true ascent was made by a British expedition lead by John Hunt in 1953. Edmund Hilary, a New Zealander, and Tensing Norgay, a Nepali Sherpa, were the first to summit and were placed into mountaineering folklore. There were subsequent ascents of Everest from other routes. Reinhold Messner, an Italian, was the first person to climb to Everest's 8848m (29,029 feet) summit without supplementary oxygen, in 1978, an amazing feat of human endurance.

I read everything I could about Everest Base Camp. But how was I going to get there?

How to admit defeat on the mountains

I walked 44 more Munros in 2014 and I was now halfway through climbing the 3000-ft peaks of Scotland. The following year, Caroline and I decided to set up our own business, and I only managed eight Munros as we were working every weekend. Phil's patience and understanding was commendable as I made my weekly Friday phone call to cancel the weekend's Munro trip.

I managed 25 Munros in 2016, but I still dreamed about Everest Base Camp. However, I was working 80 hours per week and could only get trips with Caroline at Christmas time or bank holiday weekends. How could I take 16 days off to go to the Himalayas?

*On the boat to Knoydart to celebrate Phil's last Munro.
My most enjoyable day on the hills.*

Phil was nearing the end of his Munro journey and we had some amazing trips in 2017, to little-trodden places such as Glen Affric, 15 miles west of Loch Ness, and the Knoydart peninsula on the west coast, for where we left Mallaig on a fishing boat in the dark in November to claim its two Munros.

Phil had two of the 282 Munros remaining and we decided to head to Ben More in Mull in February 2018 for his penultimate climb. The forecast was good and we booked the ferry from Oban-Craignure on a Friday morning for our first trip of the year.

The crampons and ice axe came out halfway up Ben More. Then a storm of biblical proportions hit us. The wind was in excess of 70mph, too strong to stand in. Both of us were on our hands and knees 630m from the summit, 150m in elevation. The thought of turning back so close to the summit on Phil's penultimate Munro was a painful one. We hunkered down and discussed options. We both knew we had to turn back but neither of us wanted to admit defeat. I tried to stand up and got blown 10 feet across the mountain. The decision was made: retreat and live to fight another day.

That was the worst weather either of us had ever experienced on the mountains and on reflection the day could have ended differently if we had not turned back when we did. Instead, Phil, myself and Jim Marshall got to return to Mull in April, when we camped on a beach at the bottom of the mountain, drinking whisky and having a great time.

Ben More was climbed in the clag, which meant Ladhar Bheinn in Knoydart would complete the Munros for Phil. We made the trip in May 2018 and it was amongst my best days in the hills.

We took the boat from Mallaig and summated the Munro easily, reflecting on the numerous trips we had done together and Phil's 25-year journey to this place, an amazing achievement that I hope to replicate one day.

Neither of us are big alcohol drinkers, but we had a few that evening and managed to get a lock-in in the Old Forge pub, one of the most remote in the UK, before stumbling back to the bunkhouse in the small hours.

The boat trip on the rib the next day was an exhilarating end to an amazing weekend.

Running on empty

In 2018 I climbed a further 33 Munros, including my first roped-up trip, up Liatach in Torridon, followed by six Munros on Skye, the following week. Perhaps it wouldn't be too long before I was following in Phil's footsteps, up Munro No.282. I began to consider what new challenges I could find once there were no more Munros to conquer.

A business acquaintance called Stuart MacDonald had a passion for running and this began to appeal to me, as it provided competition and a high degree of fitness. I started to train with Stuart and we entered races together. In return, I started to take him up the hills with me.

Along with James Burns, Stuart joined me on a trip to climb the Five Sisters of Kintail in Glenshiel in July 2018. We had a great day bagging the three Munros and got chatting about our bucket lists. I shared my Everest Base Camp dream. The more we spoke about it, the more I thought, 'Stuff it, you only live once!' I was going to be 40 the following year. During that conversation on the Five Sisters, I took a big step towards Everest.

I researched everything I could about getting to Base Camp and the more I read, the more convinced I became that this was something I could do. And so, in August 2018, Stuart and I booked a departure for October of the following year. God willing, we would reach Base Camp on the day of my 40th birthday, October 13. Little did I know, I was a few short months away from a crisis that would put everything into jeopardy.

I was the fittest I have ever been in the summer of 2018. Running was becoming a passion, just as hillwalking had. After competing in my first 10km race in Killin in August 2017, I had ran the Stirling half marathon in April 2018, the Skye half marathon in June and the Glasgow half marathon in September, along with numerous hill races and 10km races – as well as the aforementioned 33 Munros.

But the thing about reaching that level of fitness is, you think you can do anything. You feel invulnerable. I was also working 90 hours per week, stressed beyond belief, not sleeping and not eating enough food for someone who was training like a professional athlete.

After Ricky completed the Munros, he got bit by the running bug and was competing on the ultra-marathon circuit. These are races that are longer than the 26.2-mile marathon, generally run on remote trails and where, for the majority of participants, completion is the goal, rather than achieving a competitive time. You don't ask an ultra runner what time they ran, you ask them if they finished.

I decided that this type of racing was better suited to my mentality and love for the outdoors, rather than running around busy city centres in a more race-orientated 10km or half-marathon.

During one of my midweek bouts of insomnia I decided I was going to do an ultra marathon, and entered the Glen Ogle ultra, which was taking place on November 2.

I was running between 60 and 70km per week in training and feeling good, but just after the Glasgow half marathon I got a cold and my Grandad sadly passed away after a battle with cancer. Both knocked the stuffing out of me. Should I pull out of the ultra? After another night of counting sheep, I decided I would raise money for the hospice who cared for my Grandad in his final days. This would give me the drive to get to the start line and hopefully to the finish.

I completed the Glen Ogle race – 33 miles over numerous hills – and had a great night out with friends and family afterwards. Everyone had told me that you're tired for weeks after an ultra and you just want to eat anything you can put your hands on. I woke up the day after the race feeling fine. Two days later I ran an 8km trail in the dark, with a headtorch, and pulled a ligament in my foot. My body was telling me to slow down.

Me after completing the Glen Ogle Ultra. Little did I know this would be the catalyst to my breakdown.

Work was still manic and on the Wednesday after the race I took a dizzy turn in a meeting. I felt like I was either going to be sick or pass out. I excused myself and carried on with my day.

Caroline and I went to New York just before Christmas 2018 and I suffered a panic attack on the plane, but other than that my health was good.

However, by mid February, my body was rejecting the life I was leading: I was stressed, sleep deprived, over-trained and under-nourished. The symptoms I associated with work were now affecting my home life. I was having panic attacks in my own living room.

I was diagnosed with acute exhaustion/chronic fatigue. My recovery took months and I soon realised it would have to be holistic in nature. I was recovering from this debilitating illness, but also searching for a work-life balance and maintaining my fitness. We also had a business to run and I knew the 90-hour weeks could not continue. Caroline was my rock in all aspects of my recovery, and the business could not have kept on track without her.

I slowly worked myself back to good health over the coming months, receiving excellent help from Steven McGill, Jimmy Clarkston and James McCourt who worked on my nutrition and training; my lifestyle and what was going on inside my head.

We decided on slashing my working week from 90 hours to 50. This had the knock-on effect of freeing up all the time I needed to train and rest properly.

In terms of my psychology, the issue I needed to address was the insatiable drive that had both positive and negative effects: it propelled my professional success, but had also led to my overworking; it had fuelled my ambition to see Everest, but had also pushed me to the very edge of physical collapse.

My loyal companion Phil was also a big factor in my successful recovery and his kind words and patience ensured that I was back on the hills after a three-month absence.

Myself and Islay on my comeback walk up to the CIC hut at Ben Nevis. This was the day I knew I would be fit enough to go to Everest.

I decided to take my dog Islay up to the North Face CIC hut on Ben Nevis. It was technically just a walk, but with 800 metres of ascent it would test my fitness. Never mind Everest, I needed to see if I could still take on a Munro in the foreseeable future.

Despite 40mph icy winds, I had an amazing day. I felt as though I was back. I have never been happier on the hills.

I started focussing on the far away Munros, concentrating on trips rather than mountains. After two months or so, around mid July, I knew I was fit and healthy enough to keep my date with Everest Base Camp that autumn.

PART TWO – MY JOURNEY TO BASE CAMP

Kathmandu – Rammechap – Surkey

Stuart and I left Glasgow Airport on Thursday, October 4, 2019, bound for Dubai, where we could connect to Kathmandu, Nepal. I'm not great at sleeping on planes and I was grateful for the four-hour wait for the connection, when I managed to close my eyes.

Welcome to Nepal, Kathmandu Airport

We arrived into the chaos of Tribhuvan International Airport, Kathmandu on Friday evening. The power of good planning: Stuart had arranged our tourist visas in advance, so we skipped the long queue in arrivals, our bags came out quickly and our guide was waiting for us as we exited the airport. A seamless arrival to Nepal!

Our guide flagged us a taxi, the smallest car I have ever seen. The driver opened the boot, which had about enough space for a laptop bag never mind the two large duffle bags Stuart and I had for 16 days in Nepal. The driver decided to put the bags on the roof of the car, which had now doubled in weight, before we even got inside.

Stuart asked: "Are you going to tie the bags to the roof?"

"No," came the matter-of-fact response.

The next 30 minutes were spent racing through Kathmandu in the dark, with Stuart and I taking every opportunity, as we hurled round corners and climbed hills, to check if our belongings were still with us, or strewn across the streets behind.

I had been a little apprehensive about our accommodation during this trip as it had been a while since I had roughed it to see some hard-to-reach corner of the world. However, our hotel in the backpackers' district of Thamel was a nice surprise. We had a quick wander around the neighbourhood and settled on a local cafe for dinner. In order to reduce the risk of falling ill, we had decided to stick to a vegetarian diet for the duration of our trip, a first for me but something Stuart had been experimenting with for a number of months after working in an abattoir. After pizzas and a coke each and we both managed a good nine hours sleep – although after losing a night's sleep on the Dubai flight, I could have done with a little longer.

***

After breakfast on Saturday, we set about reducing the weight of our over-laden duffle bags from 19kg to the 10kg we were allowed to take on the trek. Without any scales, we ended up convincing ourselves that we had made the weight, even though the bags were a struggle to lift. The truth would come out at Rammechap airport.

We wandered around Kathmandu in 29 degrees, a lovely change to the autumnal cool of Scotland. Lunch was the same food, in the same place – we couldn't be too careful.

We had booked our trek through a company called Himalayan Wonders. I had been communicating with the company's representative, Raine Gorter, for over a year, and it was nice to finally meet her in person. And I had something very important to discuss with her.

We had planned to fly from Kathmandu airport to Lukla, which has been voted the most dangerous airport in the world. Lukla airport was constructed in the 1960s using money raised by Edmund Hilary, Everest's first conqueror. A month before our trip, Raine had emailed me to say that from October 1, all trekkers would have to fly from a remote airstrip in Rammechap, a five-hour rickety bus journey up a mountain pass from Kathmandu.

While Stuart and I were keen to fly into Lukla airport, that bus journey on top of our travelling to get to Nepal was not appealing to either of us. I arranged with Raine that we would get a helicopter from Kathmandu, and so avoid the bus leg of the journey. She agreed in principle on email, but had told me that she could only confirm the helicopter once we arrived in Nepal.

Even now, she could not give us the good news we were hoping for. One of the guides said the helicopters had still to be confirmed due to it being the Hindu festival of Dashain. It is celebrated every year for a total of 15 days, the most important being the first, seventh, eighth, ninth, tenth and fifteenth, one of which fell on the day before our planned helicopter flight. The guide intimated all the pilots would be out partying the night before our flight and would be in no fit state to fly the helicopters.

Raine said she would confirm the position in a few hours, but my gut was telling me the 2am rise ahead of a winding, five-hour bus journey was looking likely.

Stuart and I went out for dinner and to exchange our US dollars into Nepalese Rupees, a closed currency you can only get once in Nepal. We went for dinner in the same café (no pizza this time, we were living on the edge and ordered pasta).

We returned to the hotel at around 9.30pm and our fears were confirmed: the helicopter was no longer an option and we would be getting picked up at 2:30am the following morning. I frantically made contact with a back-up option, a company that could supply helicopters. However, the arrangements were too vague. In their worst-case scenario, we would be delayed by up to 48 hours and dropped further up the trail, catching up with our group. We wanted to do the trek in its entirety and this option felt like cheating.

Our lights went out at 10.30pm, with alarms set for 2am. A combination of excitement, nerves and dread about the bus journey resulted in both of us getting zero sleep. Maybe I should have booked the Maldives for my 40th.

After a quick shower and at least two checks of our bags, we were on the mini bus at 2.30am on Sunday morning, passing the revellers enjoying the best Dashain had to offer. Like most things you worry about, the bus journey was not as bad as anticipated; a combination of travel sickness pills and a good podcast ensured the shortened four-and-a half hour journey was far from the ordeal we had feared. At least, not for us. One of our group, Tina, who would become a great friend, spent most of the journey with her head in a bag.

We arrived at the madness of Rammechap airport at 7.30am and quickly unloaded our bags from the roof of the minibus. We then joined a queue outside a hut to check in our bags, before we learned there had been a change of plan: our guides told us to leave the bags and head into a local cafe.

A quick breakfast of cheese omelettes and a bottle of water

was hastily gulped down, before we were told to head back to the hut as our delayed flight was now ready to go. Our duffle bags were weighed and despite being 4kg over, I avoided having to pay any extra. Stuart was not so lucky but $6 was a good price for the extra clothing and supplies he had.

We scampered into the rudimentary departure room, where we were abruptly told to open our duffle bags by the security guard. He gave a cursory hand sweep of my bag. And then things got weird.

The guard asked: "Where is your lighter?"

I said: "I don't have one, I don't smoke."

He wasn't taking no for an answer and shouted in my face: "Give me your lighter!"

I shouted back in my broadest Glasgow voice: "*I don't have a lighter*!"

He accepted this and on I went, only to hear him shouting to the next unlucky passenger: "Where is your lighter?"

Never mind about the international arms race, the humble cigarette lighter is considered a weapon of mass destruction in Nepal.

In the departure area, we were once again hit with a delay. The clouds had descended upon us. As we waited, we saw four flights arrive and our spirits were lifted, but we were told these were earlier flights that had left Rammechap for Lukla and had to turn back.

Due to its elevated position at 2860m, landing at Lukla airport is a skill only a few pilots are capable of. It requires perfect timing, as the runway ends at the face of a mountain. When taking off, the end of the runway drops into an abyss thousands of feet deep. Planes only attempt to land in the best conditions. Unfortunately for us, today was not a perfect day at Lukla, despite the baking 30-degree heat in Rammechap. The flight from Rammechap to Lukla lasts only 20 minutes, but it seemed like a million miles away, as did my dream of seeing Everest.

After five hours of lying on a dusty concrete floor, melting in the afternoon heat and with over 250 people waiting for flights, our trekking company managed to secure a helicopter flight for five of our group. We were ecstatic!

Our helicopter came in to land and to the rage of the remaining passengers, the VIPs, as we called ourselves (myself, Stuart, Duncan - a solo traveller from England - Tina and Annette, both friends from Australia) were on our way to Lukla. However, as soon as the helicopter landed, it took straight off again, without us. We later found out that the helicopter had been called out for a rescue and our thoughts turned from our own disappointments to the safety of those who had been in trouble on the mountains.

Our trekking company broke the bad news that if we didn't

get a flight out in the next 90 minutes our options would be: a six-hour bus journey back to Kathmandu and a return the next day; compete with the 250 other people scrambling for the available rooms in Rammechap; or stay at a makeshift camp that was being put up near the airport. Neither option sounded appealing.

During my recovery from illness, one of my focuses had been letting go of things I can't control. Twelve months earlier, I would have been in despair in this situation. Now, despite the chaos, uncertainty and 30-degree heat, I was loving the whole experience of being miles out of my comfort zone.

We began to calculate the effect on our timeline of losing a day. Would we make it to Everest Base Camp? More importantly, would we catch our return flight home? There would be, at best, no margin for error.

Around 2.30pm, Pablo from the trekking company said, "Grab your bags". He had managed to secure us another helicopter for $250 each, to take us to Surkey. This would be a snip if it kept us on schedule.

The sting in the tail was we would have to hike five hours to our first stop, Phakding. With sunset coming at 6pm, a good part of our trek would be in darkness. I was happy with this – after all, we came to Nepal to go trekking. I had been there for two days and was itching to get started.

The five VIPs (now christened the Dream Team) made our way onto the helicopter. As we took off, it was like a scene out of the movie *Platoon,* with helicopters landing all over the airport. So much for the pilots being too drunk to fly after celebrating Dashain – they must have all sobered up by now!

*After many false starts myself getting
ready to board the helicopter.*

I've been lucky to fly in helicopters a few times and I've also had a lesson in flying one. The thing about being 5ft 4ins and 65kg is pilots like you up front, with larger people put in the back to balance the weight. It was shotgun for me! I put the headphones on and enjoyed the scenery from up front and the traffic control conversation in pidgin English.

As we approached the remote landing strip in Surkey, I could hear through the headphones that our pilot was getting very animated. I looked at him and he was sweating profusely. I looked at my fellow trekkers in the back for some reassurance, but as they didn't have headphones, they were oblivious to what was going on.

Landing in remote Surkey.

I gently tapped the pilot on the shoulder and he explained that another helicopter was taking off directly underneath us, without permission. There is no more vulnerable place to be than in a helicopter in a situation like that, and I began to fear the worst. Thankfully, however, the other helicopter turned back and we landed safely. Our bags were thrown off and we were in the middle of nowhere, perched on the edge of a mountain.

Surkey – Phakding – Namche

Our journey had officially begun, but where the hell where we? I noticed there was a hut and what looked like accommodation behind the landing strip. We went inside and had a tea before pondering what to do next. The lady serving said our guide would come and get us soon.

Off to Lukla or so we thought. We were heading straight to Phakding.

After I had been outside for some fresh air, a diminutive man arrived wearing trainers, jeans, a t-shirt and carrying a small rucksack. His name was Phurba and he would be our guide for the trek to Base Camp. At around 4.45pm, myself, Stuart, Duncan, Tina and Annette set off for Phakding, following Phurba's torch.

The first two hours of our trek were uphill and the remaining three hours a combination of ups and downs with massive drop-offs, under head torch. Thankfully, we could only hear the raging river below us and not see the drops of over 500 feet. My head torch wasn't working properly, despite new batteries. My replacement batteries were in my duffle bag, being carried by porters. It was a basic mistake and meant I had to use my phone for light.

From the start, the speed we were moving at surprised me. For months before the trip, I had trained for up to six days per week: climbing mountains, running and strength and conditioning training. I had worked with a local nutritionist to get my weight down from 75kg to my fighting weight of 65kg, and my body fat from 28% to a lean 10%. I did no climbing or running for two weeks before I left, and I rested completely for the five days prior to departure. I was in the best possible shape for 12 days of trekking. However, here I was, on day one, struggling with the pace.

We finally arrived at our accommodation in Phakding at 10pm. We were to stay at Phurba's family's teahouse. Teahouses are mountain lodges that are located along the trekking routes of Nepal. They provide the visitor with a basic level of accommodation and meals. They are similar to mountain lodges in the European Alps, but in Nepal you get private rooms and a choice of food from a menu. They are also incredibly cheap, around $5-10 per night, depending on which part of the trek you are on.

We were shattered as we had been up since 2am, and Stuart and I had lost two of the previous three nights' sleep. However, our spirits were high. It had taken us just under five hours to walk 12km with 650 metres of ascent. It had been a tough start, considering our itinerary for day one should have been an early-morning flight to Lukla and an easy three-hour walk to Phakding.

We met the four remaining members of our group: Derek from England, his son Simon also from England but living in Thailand, Nitin from India and Smita, also from India. Despite getting a later helicopter, they had been dropped straight into Lukla, saving them a two-hour uphill hike.

I had a large portion of egg fried rice which was much needed after munching my way through the last of my protein bars during the day. The See You Lodge and Restaurant teahouse had Western-style flush toilets and a shower, which we all fought over before retiring to our twin bedrooms at 11.30pm. Day two, Phakding to Namche, was 25km and 1000m of ascent. I went to bed a little concerned about whether I was fit enough to handle another 11 days of this.

I managed to sleep uninterrupted until 4am, when one of the side effects of altitude sickness tablets, the increased passing of urine, wakened me from my slumber. I had procrastinated for some time about taking the tablets. The macho side of me said I wouldn't need them, but getting to Base Camp was my dream and I decided to increase my chances of success whenever I could.

The best pills to take are Diamox, which is an Acetazolamide water diuretic pill. These help prevent acute mountain sickness (AMS) and high-altitude pulmonary edema (HAPE). You take one 125 mg tablet, twice per day, 24 hours before ascending beyond 12,000 feet and another one the day after descending from your highest point: in our case the 5364m of Everest Base Camp. All of us experienced the strange side effects of tingling in the hands and feet and urinating two or three times per hour.

I had contacted my doctor for a prescription a few months before leaving, and I had learned that I needed a rabies jab to protect me from animal bites, as we would be days away from emergency help. The rabies jab was administered over three visits at a cost of £190. I showed the tablets my doctor had given me to the private doctor administering the rabies jab and she asked if I was going to Everest in a boat. My doctor had given me tablets for travel sickness instead of altitude sickness! They did come in handy for the bus journey, mind you.

I managed another two hours sleep and woke refreshed at 6am. A quick wet-wipe bath and it was time for breakfast. I opted for a cheese omelette and paid extra for a bowl of porridge, which would be needed for the big day ahead.

A few members of the group swore by lemon, ginger and honey tea, all made with natural ingredients. I tried a mug and decided this would be my Everest Base Camp drink of choice. There would be no alcohol on this trip – the effects at altitude are four or five times stronger than at sea level, as Derek found to his cost after having one beer in Namche.

Crossing my first suspension bridge.

We set off at 8.15am and most of the morning consisted of ups and downs, spinning each of the many prayer wheels we passed, for luck. We crossed our first suspension bridge of the day. They are well constructed, but around halfway across they can be very springy. When you get off the other side it takes a few minutes to regain the sense of being on *terra firma*. To my pleasant surprise, the pace was easy; it was all about acclimatising from now on. We stopped off in the sunshine around 10.30am for some tea, which was nice surprise.

Waterfall en route to Namche.

The company was fantastic, and I now had the chance to chat

to everyone in the group, getting to know their back stories. I was grateful that we had decided to do a group trek.

I enjoyed a lunch of egg fried rice (again) and had my first experience of a long-drop toilet in Nepal. I had heard numerous stories and we had jokingly practiced how to assume the position without tumbling over. Thankfully, due to my high-carb diet, I didn't need to put the practice to use.

Along the route, literally every other house was converted into a shop selling the Everest Base Camp essentials: Mars and Snickers bars, tins of tuna, handkerchiefs and the currency of the trek, toilet rolls. Every one of us was obsessed about having enough toilet rolls as you had to provide your own in every toilet and teahouse. We always kept a roll in our day sacks and in our duffle bags, just in case.

Due to the difficulty of supplying meat to such a remote area, the Sherpas and other people who live along the trail get most of their protein from a dish called Dhal Bhat. This consists of steamed rice, lentil soup, cooked vegetables and curry, absolutely loaded with garlic. I've suffered for a number of years with irritable bowel syndrome and intolerance to garlic, which meant Dal Bhat was off the menu for me. Most of our group wolfed it down at lunch and dinner time. Phubar, our guide, coined the phrase "24 hour Dal Bhat power" as he and the other guides ate it twice per day. It certainly gave them the energy they needed to power along the trails.

The Sherpa people are one of the ethnic groups native to mountainous regions in Nepal and Himalaya. Historically they were a nomadic people, with their roots in any of four different clans, which over time split into the 20 clans that exist today.

Entering the Sagamatha National Park

A study by UCLA at Berkeley identified 30 genetic factors that make Sherpa's bodies suited to high altitude environments, including EPAS1, which enables their bodies to adapt quickly to high altitude. EPAS1 is known as the "super athlete" gene, which regulates the body's production of haemoglobin, allowing for greater efficiency in the use of oxygen. Dhal Bhat helps, too.

The Sherpa people have been working with climbers trying to summit the high mountains of Himalaya for over 100 years. They are renowned for their hardiness, climbing ability and knowledge of the region.

The most famous Sherpa is Tenzing Norgay, who in 1953, along with Edmund Hilary, became the first person to stand on the summit of the highest point on earth, Mount Everest. When we stopped at a village further along the trail we were lucky to meet Phu Tashi, a Sherpa who had summited Everest a whopping 12 times. I was in awe of him; I felt like I had met a rock star.

Our day-two destination, Namche, was a three-hour steep uphill trek away after lunch. I was going to need all the energy from my egg fried rice.

We had followed the glacial melt river of Dudh Koshi for just over an hour and as we turned a corner we were greeted by the knee-trembling site of the Hilary suspension bridge, 125 metres above us. I had read everything I could about the trail and this was one of the highlights I had been looking forward to. The old bridge, below the current one, was out of action. We climbed up to the bridge and waited for 15 minutes to allow the various yak and donkey trains to pass, carrying vital supplies to the towns further up the trail.

Due to a lack of roads, all supplies to the towns on the trails have to be carried by yak, donkey or humans. We saw some incredible loads being carried on porters' backs; later in the trek, we saw one carrying a 110kg fridge up the trail. The porters moved at two or three times the speed we did, they were absolute machines.

First sight of the Hilary suspension bridge.

As we readied to cross the Hilary bridge, Stuart, Duncan, Simon and I hatched a plan. At the risk of losing our phones to the foaming river below, we decided to cross as a foursome, turning around on the springy bridge to take each other's photo, a novel keepsake from what was proving to be an amazing start to the trek.

Phurba stopped at the park ranger's office to pay for our permits and we arrived in the town of Namche at 4.45pm. It had been a great day and although I had felt tired during the final 30 minutes of the trek, I was in great fettle. I felt strong and fit for the days that lay ahead.

Namche would be the last bastion of semi-civilisation for the next seven days. The town is built in a bowl shape, with an elevation of 3440m at its lowest point, and it has a population of over 1600. There are shops, bars and a hairdresser (more about that later in the trip). As we passed through the town, we saw an official North Face store, an Irish bar and all types of shops selling outdoor clothing, both fake and genuine brands. I had found my ideal holiday destination.

Our accommodation for the evening was at one of the highest points in the town. Just an extra bit of training, I told my aching body.

I paid $5 for a shower, which was in a hut with the shower head taped to the ceiling by gaffer tape. Still, the water was warm and I managed to shave my face and head and get a good wash after a long, dusty day on the trail.

We met for dinner at 7pm, back onto pizza, a rare full-fat Coke and a mint tea (tea was free with every meal). Duncan ordered an apple pie for dessert, which was all the encouragement Stuart and I needed to join him. We had walked 28 km, climbed 1070m and burned 2200 calories; anything would have tasted good after that!

Arriving in cloudy Namche

After dinner, Phurba gave his daily speech. He went from being a joker to the most serious person you could meet. Later, we used to laugh at these nightly chats. He was a great guy and a patient leader.

He said we would have to drink at least four litres of water per day to prevent altitude sickness. If we felt a headache coming, we had to drink as much as possible.

I popped another Diamox tablet before bed, knowing that from now on, altitude sickness would be our greatest enemy.

Acclimatisation Day at Namche

I slept for eight-and-a-half hours, not even waking when Stuart got up for the toilet at 2am. At breakfast none of us were feeling or looking great, myself included. Derek had decided he wanted a beer after dinner and now said it felt like he had drank ten. I resisted the desire to call him a "one can Dan" knowing that I could barely handle two at sea level. I forced down a cheese omelette, a hearty bowl of porridge and, of course, a mug of lemon, ginger and honey tea.

Today was to be an 'easy' acclimatisation day.

Just as I was packing my bag to leave, Annette shouted from downstairs for me to rush down. I quickly realised that at altitude, nothing moves fast. However, I hurried downstairs, following her and Tina outside and up some steep steps, to be greeted by the sun lighting up a snow-capped mountain. My spirits were lifted. Our views the day before had been restricted by cloud, but this was what I had came to see. Away from the stress of work, and faced with such magnificent natural beauty, my day seemed wonderfully simple. Here, all I needed was the will and the fitness to put one foot in front of the other.

The hike out of the village was steep and got my heart rate up. We emerged at the Everest museum, which is based at the top of a steep hill in the Sagamartha National Park. There is a viewpoint with breathtaking views of Nuptse, Lhotse, Ama Dablam and the mighty Everest. Once again, though, the weather wasn't playing ball: there were over 100 people 'oohing' and 'ahhing' when the cloud cleared for a second, before again covering the prize. We stood with our necks craned back for half an hour without success.

Tenzing Norgay Statue

I took some photographs of the statue of Tenzing Norgay and had a wander around the museum. I could have been in a museum in any city in the world, but I was in one of the remotest parts of the planet, days from motorised transport and civilisation.

The next 500m climb was extremely steep and the altitude was affecting most of the group. I was feeling really strong; the months of training were paying off and a good night's sleep had given me the best possible start. I tried my best to stay as close to our leader Phurba, who was gliding up the hill effortlessly. We reached a cairn perched on a cliff with a steep drop off and got some amazing photos, despite the cloud doing its best to ruin them. I did my signature outstretched-arm pose, which I do on top of all the mountains I climb, much to the amusement of the rest of the group.

Signature pose

Near the top of the route we met a gentleman called Tommy Gustafsson, who was setting up a conservation project for the Sagamartha National Park, called Sagamartha Next. The region has over 50,000 visitors per year, all contributing waste and rubbish. With no real means of getting the waste removed or recycled it is currently burned, which is not great for the environment. The project aims to create sustainable trekking and tourism in the area. Tommy asked that when we left Namche at the end of the trek, could we manage to take a 1kg bag of recyclable goods back to Lukla? This would be the equivalent of the amount of waste and recycling we would create after 12 days on the trail. This great cause was only in its infancy during our trek and I am sure it will grow in the years ahead.

At 3775 metres. Every day was going to get higher.

Now we had a choice: to stop at the Panorama Hotel or continue further up to the Everest View Hotel, or as we called it the 'Everest No View Hotel'. After a brief discussion with Phurba, we all agreed the extra training and climb up to 3880m would benefit our acclimatisation. This would mark the highest point I had climbed – from now on, I would be continually climbing higher and higher than I ever had before.

We sat outside on the hotel's balcony. In the cloud, the difference in temperature was noticeable. Caps were replaced by hats and my gloves came out for the first time on the trip. We had lemon, ginger and honey tea and some cookies, which tasted very much like Scottish shortbread, a nice reminder of home. And we wondered how the hotel got its name: all we could see was cloud.

Looking down on Namche

All that was left to finish the day was a steep downhill hike to Namche. I was feeling physically and mentally strong and was having a great time. Things were literally on the up. But when would we see Everest?

We got back to the teahouse at the early hour of 2pm. I had a nice lunch of egg fried rice (again) and opted for mint tea this time.

Myself, Stuart and Duncan quickly left our bags and went exploring Namche. North Face sell t-shirts with the co-ordinates and name of the town/city for most of their shops worldwide. My brother-in-law Stephen has taken to collecting these. I popped in and bought two with Namche on it, one for me and one for him – it's not one you could get online. They cost £45 each, but it was the least I could do for the person who had introduced me to the mountains in the first place.

When I opened my duffle bag, I discovered that my razor had broken from the handle. After a quick scout around Namche, I found a chemist. I am renowned for my milk-bottle-white skin and to prevent sunburn I plaster factor 50 all over my face and neck when out hillwalking. I have been known to get sunburn on the coldest of days. My shaven head and the rest of my body are covered in clothes, regardless of the weather. Now, after our first few days had been bright and sunny, I was concerned I would run out of sun cream. With Namche being my last chance to buy some, I negotiated a price of £30 for a single-use razor, 100ml of sun cream and a small bottle of hand sanitiser. I must brush up on my negotiation skills. After meeting up with Stuart and Duncan, I proudly showed off my purchases. Duncan quickly pointed out that I don't have dark Asian skin, which the sun cream bottle stated it was suitable for! I went back to exchange it and walked out £10 lighter. Chemist staff in Namche are not daft.

Stuart spotted a laundrette and took our dirty washing away with the promise of retrieving them clean and dry the next day. Knowing you had clean underwear and tops to wear most days was a great morale booster, especially when the going got tough later in the trip. In retrospect I would have taken fewer clothes and I would have replaced the weight with protein powder and porridge oats to help balance out my diet. Such was my craving for protein that I was literally chasing live chickens by day four.

After an extended shower and another shave of my face and head it was time for dinner. I went a bit crazy and opted for macaroni, pasta and vegetables, another delicious meal. The teahouse set up is very efficient. The guide takes your food order and serves it to you. He keeps a note of any extras that you have to pay for, such as bottled water, showers, phone charging, Wi-Fi and extra food, which is settled up before leaving. The cost for water varied for us. Lower down on the trail it was around $2.50 for a litre bottle, rising to $5 in Gorak Shep, a pittance when you think a porter has carried this for four or five days for your pleasure. Wi-Fi, showers and phone charging prices increased similarly the higher up the trail you got.

The owner of the shop at the Killin Outdoor Centre had recommended a Grayl Geopress water filter that he has used on his own expeditions in the Himalayas. I also took chlorine tablets, but the combination of bottled water with the filter sufficed. The water was tap water that had been treated and I felt more secure using the filter.

In between courses at dinner, I got chatting to an Indian gentleman who had just returned from Base Camp. He shared some stories of his adventure and my sense of excitement was off the scale! I had been taking each day at a time, not thinking about the prize of achieving my lifetime's ambition to reach Base Camp. Now it seemed so close, but there was a long way to go.

After the main course, the two Australian ladies in our group, Annette and Tina, produced a birthday cake for me, although my 40th birthday was still four days away. Phurba warned us in our after-dinner talk that people start dropping out from now on, due to how tough the trek gets. When I was blowing out my candle, I made a wish that all of us would make it to Base Camp.

After eating my cake, we were presented with a new member of our group: Relly from Java, Indonesia. Relly had not made it onto a helicopter like the rest of our group and had to wait until the next day to catch a flight to Lukla, and had been a day behind us as a result. He had spent his first two days with a group of Japanese youngsters. We saw them most days and they were the happiest bunch of people I had ever met. I christened them the 'giggle squad' as they were always laughing and in good spirits.

Relly's English wasn't great, but his smiling face and amenable nature were good additions to our group. I got chatting to Relly after a few days and I learned that he had spent the previous three weeks exploring Everest from the

North Tibetan side. Everest is best seen in all its glory from the Tibetan side as it is hidden by its neighbouring peaks from the Nepalese route we were taking. His photographs were amazing. Rather than trekking the route, he had gone up by an organised bus tour. The bus was pumped full of oxygen to prevent his group getting altitude sickness, as were the tents they stayed in at night. An interesting take on exploring Everest and possibly an alternative to explore on another occasion.

Our group was now 10: Relly; Derek from Nottingham; his son Simon, now residing in Kaengkhoi, Thailand; Tina and Annette from Geelong, near Melbourne; Duncan from Worcester, England; Smita from Mumbai, India; Nitin from Bangalore, India; and Stuart and myself from sunny Scotland. A great mix of people and cultures.

Duncan had been going on about getting a deep-fried Mars bar for days and was shocked to discover myself and Stuart had never tried one. According to Duncan, it was a staple of the Scottish diet! Duncan decided to order one on this evening, only to discover the contents of an apple pie inside the pastry. His face was a picture and the whole group revelled in his misfortune. Duncan was a great character throughout the trek and the two of us got on great.

Namche – Phortse

Day four was going to be a tough day hiking the less traditional route of Namche to Phortse, with some significant descents and ascents, which would hopefully help with our acclimatisation. This would avoid the worst of the crowds who were heading via Tengboche on the opposite side of the valley. I was looking forward to seeing the monastery in Tengboche; Phurba assured us we would catch it on the way back.

We decided on an early night – I hit the hay around 9.30pm and fell straight asleep. I awoke at 11.30pm and was awake until 4:30 due to a combination of insomnia and a painful stomach ache caused by garlic in my lunch. I took a mental note to make sure I asked for all of my meals to be free from garlic. I would say to Phurba before every meal: "NO GARLIC." This included my order for porridge every morning. Considering the amount of garlic the Nepalese eat, I wouldn't be surprised if they put it in porridge.

***

Our doors were knocked at 6.30am and we were greeted by a new face. Mingmau would join Phurba as our guide for the remainder of the trip. Mingmau's English wasn't great and this restricted his career development as a Sherpa guide, but his smiling face, excellent customer service skills and caring nature were welcome. He was slender in height and build, but the strongest and fittest man I have ever met. He would run ahead of the group if he saw a yak train coming and would not be remotely out of breath, while the rest of the group huffed and puffed, walking at a snail's pace behind him.

From the moment I woke, everything was a struggle for me, from brushing my teeth to putting my contact lenses in. I noticed my resting heart rate was now over 100 (it usually sits around 50). The effects of altitude were starting to tell. Suddenly, I didn't feel as cocky about making it to Base Camp. The realisation that this would be a mental challenge, as much as a physical one, dawned.

I struggled to force down my breakfast of porridge and a cheese omelette. Even the lemon, ginger and honey tea wasn't working its magic.

After that, I walked from the restaurant across to my room and I was stopped in my tracks by the view. I was surrounded by 6000m peaks bathed in morning sunshine. It was cold and frosty at ground level, but I could tell it was going to be a beautiful day and my mood lifted instantly.

We prepared our bags every morning before breakfast. They were then collected by our porters, usually young guys varying in age from 16 to 20. This would be a plumb job for local youngsters, which would hopefully lead to well-paid roles as guides or porters in the future. My duffle bag weighed around 15kg and Stuart's was around 20kg. One porter would carry both bags on his back every day and generally arrived at the next destination 4 or 5 hours before us, despite only wearing sandals and a light jacket. We only saw them for a few minutes each day, but Phurba said we would have an opportunity to socialise and thank them at the end of the trip. I was looking forward to that. I appreciated their efforts every day while I struggled with my 7kg rucksack.

We set off up the steep steps leading out of Namche at around 7.30am. As we looked down on the bowl-shaped village, we realised this would be our last view of civilisation for six days.

Our pace would be slow to allow us to acclimatise. This was also great for my current tired state. I just wanted to get to Phortse and catch up with some sleep. The early trekking went well and we were warming up nicely in the morning sun.

Then, after a few hours on the trail, it finally happened: our first view of Everest! I was so happy, I could feel my eyes welling up with tears: it had been such a long journey to get here. It was the gift that kept on giving – around every corner we got a better view of Ama Dablam, Lhotse and, unmistakeable, with the jet stream cloud about it, the mighty Everest.

The sky was bright blue and the sun was high. We walked along the trail and passed various Buddhist Stupas. These are commemorative monuments containing relics, which are sometimes used as places of meditation. They are a lovely sight in such a remote area.

My first sight of Everest. Hidden in the cloud.

Our lunch stop was a new high for me at 3970m. When we were about 10 minutes away, Derek had an immediate call to nature. Our instruction to maintain a modest pace was suddenly abandoned: I've never seen an Englishman move so fast at altitude. Derek went sprinting up the last 200 metres and managed to relieve himself without incident!

Lunch was in a nice restaurant perched on top of a steep cliff. The views were amazing, although the structure didn't look particularly robust. You learn that things that would concern you in the west don't mean much in Nepal, you just roll with the punches. I'd struggle to make a living in Nepal selling health and safety PPE. Judging by my hiking efforts, I wouldn't make much of a guide either.

I ate vegetable fried rice, an experimental choice. I purchased some more bottled water and after a quick filter, we were off. The next 90 minutes were downhill, the descent was very steep. I found my experience of hill walking back home helped with my foot placement and we were at the bottom of the valley in no time. We crossed a bridge and all that was left was a steep 275m ascent to the village of Phortse. I was still feeling physically strong, but tiredness was getting the better of me. I put some dance tunes on. It seemed to make the hike go more quickly and the cheesy music certainly gave us all a laugh.

At 3950m, the village of Phortse is not part of the main trekking circuit and resembles a traditional Sherpa village. It only received electricity in 2003 and is famed for its farming. As we walked through the village to our accommodation, we saw many farmers ploughing their fields barefoot, swinging sharp ploughs without a care in the world. I had noticed on the trek into Phortse that, while the local people generally wore traditional clothing, they all seemed to have the latest designer puffer jackets from brands such as Mountain Equipment, Mountain Hardwear and so on. It transpires that

Phortse's population includes more than a few high-altitude climbers and over 75 Everest summiteers – amazing for a village with a population of just under 300. The climbers bring back the jackets and expedition gear from their climbs, hence the super-cool farmers!

There is a world-class climbing facility in Phortse called the Khumbu Climbing Centre, where a team of climbers teach Sherpas essential skills and teacher training courses, so the Sherpas can pass the knowledge on to others.

Tragically on April 25, 2015, a 7.8 magnitude earthquake struck Nepal, killing almost 9000 people. The damage was felt throughout the country, from Kathmandu deep into the Khumbu valley, where we were trekking, destroying villages. It reached as far as Everest Base Camp, killing 22 climbers in an avalanche. Seventeen days later another earthquake struck, this time of 7.3 magnitude. The disaster caused damage of over $10 billion, half of Nepal's GDP. Many families lost both loved ones and their homes. Phortse was almost destroyed and the trekking tourist trade, which accounts for $120 million per year to the Nepalese economy, was decimated.

Thankfully when we arrived in 2019, the locals seemed to have recovered from the tragedy and there was no mention of the natural disaster. The resilient Sherpa people seemed to be back to their normal lives. However, as I write this in the middle of the global Covid 19 pandemic, the Nepalese and Sherpa people are once again struggling. Tourism has disappeared and without a strong welfare system there is mass unemployment and widespread hardship. The company we booked the trip with, Himalayan Wonders, are involved in a Go Fund Me initiative to help the guides tidy up the trail, ensuring they receive an income in this difficult time, something I happily contributed to.

As was becoming the norm, our accommodation was at the furthest point in the village. The cloud had dropped, as had the temperature, and we were glad to reach our base for the evening, the Guesthouse Tashi Friendship Lodge. We had hiked for 13km, with 900m of ascent, an easy Munro day back home, but it had felt more like 10 Munros at this altitude.

Despite the accommodation being basic, the rooms and the dining room were warm. Outside it was below freezing and it was only going to get colder from now on.

I put my phone and watch in for a charge, paid for a shower and Wi-Fi and settled into my room. I had brought a power pack with me, which I was told would give me around nine charges of my phone and watch. I would keep this for later in the trek, when electricity would be more scarce.

I had been looking forward to my shower, but when I jumped in, I found that the control was more than a little temperamental. The temperature would race to a scalding heat, but then a slight nudge of the dial would send it plummeting to near freezing. I was screaming from the hot water one second and yelping out of an icy stream the next. In the middle of this battle of extremes, the LPG generator powering the unit failed and I was standing in total darkness, unable to locate the infernal temperature dial and covered in soap. I rinsed off as quickly as I could, and changed for dinner.

Duncan finally got his deep-fried Mars bar. He thoroughly enjoyed it, but I couldn't see the appeal; it didn't look or smell very appetising to me.

At our after-dinner meeting, Phurba told us that our next destination would be Dingboche, after a tough eight-hour day on the trail. Tonight was the first night we would have our resting heart rate and oxygen levels measured. This would be a daily occurrence from now on as we would be above 4000m for the next five days. My reading was a resting heart rate of 83, higher than my usual but expected, and 91% oxygen. The heart rate would not be a major concern going forward, as your heart beats faster and harder to circulate the thicker red blood cells produced at altitude, but the oxygen levels were critical. Phurba said if any of us dipped to 70% or below, we would need to be evacuated by helicopter. Or, as Mingmau called them, the Khumbu taxis.

Phortse – Dingboche

Day five started a lot colder than the previous days. We soon got moving and reached the top of the village, where we were greeted by the warmth of the morning sun. We bumped into another group with the same plan of avoiding the crowds of the trail by staying in Phortse. We reached a cairn with Thamserku dominating the backdrop. We were now entering big mountain country. Everywhere you looked there were snow-capped peaks over 6000m.

*It was a cold start but the sun soon came up
and the views were amazing.*

Next up was a narrow ridge walk of over 3km, with 1000-feet drop-offs to the right-hand side. That certainly woke us up. I was concerned for Stuart as he has a debilitating fear of heights, but I was impressed by his desire to get the job done and he never complained once. Stuart hatched the idea of putting our towels on the back of our rucksacks to dry in the sun – a great idea, even if we looked like superheroes for the morning.

The mesmerising Ama Dablam. The group and my favourite mountain.

We continued along the ridge for around three hours and dropped into the village of Pangboche for our usual morning tea stop. We stopped at the Trekkers Holiday Inn teahouse, slightly less luxurious than the Holiday Inn chain back home but a welcome break, nonetheless. I visited a not-so-nice outdoor long-drop toilet and wondered what all the leaves were on the floor. I quickly sussed out that these were the means of compost. Thankfully, I had alcohol hand gel with me; there would be no running water on the trek from now on.

After our tea stop, the views opened up to reveal Ama Dablam, a jaw-droopingly beautiful mountain. Although not the highest, at 6812m, the entire group agreed it was the most stunning of all the mountains we saw on the trail. Ama Dablam translates as 'Mother's Necklace'. The long ridges on each side resemble the arms of a mother (Ama) protecting her child, and the hanging glacier (Dablam) is the traditional pendant containing pictures of the gods, worn by Sherpa women. Ama Dablam is often referred to as the Matterhorn of the Himalayas, after the equally stunning Swiss mountain (and another on my bucket list). Ama Dablam was first climbed in 1961 by Mike Gill from New Zealand and Barry Bishop from the USA. This beautiful mountain would dominate our views for the next few days.

The afternoon trek would be tough, taking us up into the village of Dingboche, at an altitude of 4400m. The afternoon cloud rolled in quickly, covering the mountains from view. We would get used to this in the days ahead.

All supplies are carried up by yak or human in the Khumbu region

When we arrived at our accommodation, we realised that the home comforts were slowly disappearing. Perhaps the first few days had spoiled us for what lay ahead, but as the luxuries fell away, the sense of adventure grew.

The village of Dingboche is powered mainly by solar panels. Yak dung was stuck to the side of every building or rock, drying out for use in the stoves to heat the teahouses. The village is a popular stop-off on the Everest trekking route, along with a staging post for climbers attempting Ama Dablam and Island Peak. Everything has to be brought up by yak or porter. As a result, prices were double those at our previous stops.

I went with my usual purchase of water, Wi-Fi and a shower and checked into my freezing room. I was surprised to find an en suite and even more surprised that the only means of flushing the toilet was to fill up a used coffee tin from a 90-litre bucket of water and pour it down the toilet. A first for me. I'm not precious, but the room was pretty dirty and I doubt it had ever been cleaned. 'All part of the experience,' I told myself, as I remembered we would be here for the next two nights.

I was third in line for my purchased 'hot shower'. Each time someone got in, the owner of the teahouse would wait a few minutes, then turn off the gas bottle which heated the shower. It was funny until you realised it was going to be the same for you. I jumped into the coldest shower I have ever had. He must have turned the bottle off before I got in. It was pitch black and the only light came from the LED light on the shower, which showed a reading of 32 degrees. That's the freezing point of water in Fahrenheit, so I can only assume this unit was working on that scale.

I was so cold and confused that I put my dirty clothes back on in the darkness and only realised when I got back to my room. I was sure I was never stepping foot inside a shower for the rest of the trek. I quickly changed into clean clothes and put my down jacket on. After warming up a little, I was glad to be clean and couldn't rule out running the gauntlet again the next day. It's amazing what the cold and heat can do to your mind-set.

We met for dinner around 7pm, each of us with our own story about the lack of cleanliness in the rooms and tales from the 32-degree shower. I ordered a mushroom pizza, which was not the best but it filled a gap. I noticed a change of mood in the group. Most of the team were in bed by 8pm now. Derek, Duncan, Stuart and myself were the night owls: up until 9pm.

Before bed, we got our oxygen and heart rate measured again. My resting heart rate was 91 and I gave a reading of 92% oxygen, a clean bill of health. Tomorrow would be a rest and acclimatisation day, climbing up to a high point of 4700m before heading straight back down. We would also get a long lie, meeting for breakfast at 8am. Three days until Everest Base Camp. I could almost smell the prize. Or maybe that was the burning yak dung.

***

Day six started with a bad headache. The room temperature had dropped below freezing. I got up during the night to put my hat on, but anything outside my -15 rated sleeping bag was cold. I had spent the previous nights cooking inside my Rab sleeping bag, but I was grateful for it now.

I put the headache down to a mixture of a head cold and mild altitude sickness. My mind was made up: no more freezing showers until I get back to Namche!

I spoke to Phurba about my headache, as he reminded us every day to report any change in our health. He checked my stats and my heart rate was up to 96, and my oxygen had dropped to 82%. Phurba told me to drink two litres of water and after hiking up to 4700m I would feel better. I felt as though I could barely hike up the stairs to breakfast, but I trusted our guide.

I popped a full diamox tablet. I had been taking half a tablet twice per day until now. I was not sure if they were curing me or killing me. I had experienced all the associated side effects: insomnia, lucid dreams, tingling in my feet and hands and loss of appetite. I wanted to give myself every chance of reaching Base Camp.

A reminder of home at the Dingboche snooker hall.

We left the busy village at around 9.30am, walking slowly to the trail. We passed some shops, a bakery and amazingly a snooker hall, with Scottish snooker legend Stephen Hendry on the sign outside. For such a small country, Scotland has left quite a mark on the world. For the first time I felt a little homesick, but nothing was going to keep me from my challenge now.

High above Dingboche with Mingmau. A fantastic guide and great human being.

We climbed for a couple of hours up the steep trail above the village, with the views getting better by the minute. I could see a change in the terrain; the trail was much drier and dustier now, almost desert-like. Phurba told us to cover our mouths with our buffs to stop the famous Khumbu cough caused by the dry, dusty air.

We stopped at the top of the hill and enjoyed the views,

taking some beautiful photographs. Mingmau pointed out our route for tomorrow, across the high plateau. I could see a yak train on the route, it looked otherworldly. To think we would be doing that tomorrow, just two days from Everest Base Camp.

Great spot for a photograph

I realised my two-litre water bladder had been drunk dry, a sure sign I had been dehydrated when I woke up, hence the headache. I had added Active Root sports electrolytes to my pack. I had trialled it during long runs back home and it is famed for reducing stomach aches as it contains natural ginger. And it also tastes great. I used this every day on the trail, mixed with water.

I was feeling great now. Duncan and I spotted a photo opportunity on an outstretched bit of rock with an amazing view of Ama Dablam behind. We took some incredible photos and within minutes there was a queue forming at the bottom of the rock. We should have charged people to use our spot!

Phurba told us we would have the rest of the afternoon to ourselves to rest and explore, but he advised against napping at altitude as we would wake up feeling groggy. On the way back into the village we passed the bakery again. Outside was a chalkboard sign advertising a showing of the movie *Everest* at 2pm.

We went back to the teahouse for lunch and headed up to the coffee shop for the afternoon movie. Myself, Stuart, Duncan, Nitin, Annette, Tina, Derek and Simon squeezed into a small hut along with around 50 other trekkers. If you spent over 500 Rupees, you could watch the film for free and get your phone charged: cheaper than the 500 Rupees to charge your phone at the guest house.

It was amazing to watch the movie, seeing the stars crossing the Hilary Bridge and following the route to Namche and beyond. It gave us a sense of achievement as to how far we had already come and a perspective on how far we had still to go to get to Base Camp. Just getting there was hard enough for us, let alone climbing to the summit of Everest!

After last night's freezing shower, both Stuart and I opted for a wet wipe wash in our rooms. A few years ago, I had been basking in five-star resorts in the Caribbean and this experience would have been inconceivable to me. It was a moment to reflect on the changes I had made and how exhilarating it all was for me.

The only sinister moment on the trip was an altercation I had with the owner of the teahouse in Dingboche. I've travelled all over the world, staying in luxurious and not-so-luxurious accommodation. Instead of the key cards that most places use for room access these days, this teahouse had an extremely large weighted key ring on the key for my room. Rather than take the key ring on the trail with me, I had left it in the room, taking the key with me. Unbeknown to me, that 90-gallon drum for flushing the toilet had to be refilled every day. Stuart had asked the owner to fill the drum before we left and shouted for me to give the owner the key.

As I passed him the key, he started shouting that I had lost the key ring. I explained that I had left it in the room as I didn't want to carry it. This didn't calm him down at all – he was going crazy. I'm an extremely placid person, but this idiot was boiling my blood. I managed to diffuse the situation and we went up the hill on our trek. When we returned for lunch, he shouted across the packed room: "Thamserku!" This was the name of my room, after the mountain we saw coming out of Phortse. I squeezed by everyone at my table and walked over to him. When I got there, he asked what I wanted. I said my room key, to which he replied: "What room key?"

I've been around the block a few times and met bullies like this fool before. Now everyone was laughing and he was enjoying the attention as I stood in the middle of the dining room looking like a class A idiot. I asked for the key and he dismissed me with his hand. I realised that there is only one way to deal with a bully. I pinned him against the wall and asked again for my key, using a few expletives along the way. He gave me the key, looking rather sheepish, and was warned that, had he spoke to me the way he did in Glasgow, he would not be standing for long!

As far as I was concerned the issue was done with and I calmly walked back to my seat. The dining room was in silence and my group were in shock that this quiet wee guy from Scotland had gone crazy on the bully. Never mess with an angry Scotsman.

Once I had calmed down, I felt quite bad about the situation. However, I felt vindicated when everyone from our group said the guy had been a complete idiot and our stay there was the worst of the trip. He had been overcharging people for water and Wi-Fi (I paid 500 rupees for each and Stuart was charged 700 rupees for the same things). I think there is a pretty good chance I'll be staying somewhere else next time. Despite this one experience, I have nothing but good things to say about the Nepalese people and everyone we met on the trek.

After another dinner of egg fried rice (hopefully without the owner adding any extras) Phurba told us we would be hiking for seven hours the following day, when we would all feel the debilitating effects of the increased altitude. We would be visiting the Everest Memorial, which has cairns and monuments dedicated to all who have died on Mount Everest, including those portrayed in the movie *Everest* we had watched earlier in the day, which is based on the real life events around the 1996 Mount Everest disaster, when eight people lost their lives during a fierce blizzard.

My stats tonight: a resting heart rate of 93 beats per minute and oxygen levels up to 87%. All good with just two days to go to Everest Base Camp.

Dingboche – Lobuche

Day seven would take us over 5000m above sea level. It started with a cheese omelette. This was more of a problem than you might think.

My need for calories was going up, but my appetite was disappearing. This is a common dilemma at these altitudes – despite knowing that you need to eat more and more each day, you simply have no will to do so. At this stage in the trek,

I was burning 2500 calories per day and I needed another 2000 on top of this just to survive. However, I was lucky if I was eating 1500 calories per day and that was a recipe for disaster.

We climbed up and over the high plateau we had been to the previous day. Below us to our left was the route that would lead us back to civilisation in a few days. There was so much to see, and so much to achieve before then.

Lobuche: 1 day to go.

We followed a glacial melt river before crossing it and reaching the village of Thukla, which would be our lunch stop. I went for something a bit more palatable: fried egg, hash browns and cheese, something I would never eat back home but I as looked up at the climb we faced that afternoon, I knew I had to load up on calories.

At the brow of the steep climb, we emerged at the Everest Climber's Memorial. The sun was shining but there was an icy wind. We had some time to explore and pay our respects to the climbers who had perished on Everest. I found a quiet spot out of the wind and in the warmth of the sun and thought about those poor people who had shared my obsession with this mountain and had made this same journey, never to return home.

Behind my sunglasses, tears streamed down my face. I do not get emotional like that – it's a source of humour for those who know me well – but this moment of quiet reflection was a turning point in my relationship with Everest.

For years, Caroline had begged me not to make the trek to Base Camp: not because she thought the expedition was especially perilous in itself, but because she suspected it was not an end goal, but a staging post; a scouting mission for a future attempt on the summit. And she was right. Even if I had never expressed it, this was the inevitable conclusion of my fascination with the mountain and my seemingly perpetual desire to find the next goal.

Caroline had been unhappy when I had first told her of my intention to come here. She had begged me to change my mind, and only relented when I explained that this was my life's ambition. Then she had supported me fully, even paying the deposit for the trip herself. Now, standing here, thinking about the people who had been lost on the mountain, and the loved ones they left behind, I realised I could never risk putting Caroline in that situation. My love for her was greater than my love of the mountains – even this one. It was a moment in which my life changed.

We continued along the pass to our next destination, Lobouche, at an altitude of 5030m above sea level. It shares its name with several high peaks in the region: Lobuche Far East; Lobuche East and Lobuche West, all easier to pronounce than the Gaelic-named mountains of Scotland. Tomorrow's objective, Everest Base Camp, was now a mere 8.5 km away.

Our accommodation was primitive. We were all pretty tired now and stayed in the dining area at the risk of going to bed and falling asleep before dinner. My head cold had gotten worse and I was coughing and sneezing constantly, while trying to hide my condition from Mingmau and Phurba. Today had been tough; tomorrow would be tougher, but nothing was going to stop me getting to Base Camp.

We had two hours to spare before our dinner at the earlier-than-usual time of 6.30pm. I ordered a tube of Pringles and a bottle of full-fat coke. I was desperate to get some sugar and salt in me and any calories possible at this stage. The Pringles came in at $8, but when I opened the tube, I discovered they were broken into tiny pieces. I was annoyed at this, but I had reason to reflect on this reaction a few days later. On our route back down the mountain, I met a porter carrying the largest load I had seen. I asked him what he was carrying up the mountain and he told me his load was 240 tubes of Pringles. It took him four days to carry these all the way from Lukla to Lobuche, sleeping on the trail with them. I felt ashamed at my reaction, and humbled by this man's efforts, and I was reminded once more that everything from fuel to food must make its way up the trail by porter or yak.

The showers were ice-cold and I wasn't about to make that mistake again, so I had another wet wipe wash. At home, I take two showers every day, I'm kind of obsessed with shaving and being clean cut. It was liberating to let all that go, and as everyone else was in exactly the same situation, there was no standard to which you had to conform. The smells of the trail were bad body odour, yak dung and kerosene cooking fuel. And the sensory assault did not stop there. The porters would overtake you at rapid speed playing their Nepalese music. At the time I found it annoying, but now it seems like a fond memory, something else to cherish from a trip I will remember forever.

I blamed the Pringles when I only managed half of my vegetarian pizza, but the truth is the altitude was hitting me hard, and I knew it was the same for all of our group. We were a day away from Base Camp. It seemed too close to escape us now, but Phurba warned that the following day would be our toughest test yet

Lobuche – Gorak Shep – Everest Base Camp – Gorak Shep

Sunday, October 13. My 40th birthday and my date with destiny.

I awoke in the dark of our freezing room at 4.30am. The combined effects of my cold and the altitude hit me hard, but as I wiped the ice off of the window, I could see a snow-covered peak. That was enough to get my juices flowing. And I had to put on a brave face.

*After scraping away the ice I was greeted
with this amazing sight.*

I knew that if Phurba or Mingmau had any doubt about any of our health we would be pulled out and sent back down the trail. This was repeated to us every day. A drop of 200m is usually enough to combat the effects of mild altitude sickness at this height, but an ascent of over 400m in a day can trigger the condition. With the timeframe we were operating under, the equation was simple: if someone got sick, they would not reach Base Camp. There was no way I was telling anyone I wasn't feeling well.

All wrapped up for my date with destiny.

I opened my birthday card from Caroline. She had promised me lots of gifts on my return and a few months earlier had bought me a Rolex watch. It had been a great year, during which ambitions had been fulfilled. Inside the card, there was a pouch with a key ring that was inscribed with the words: 'I love you more than the miles between us.' This was enough for me to turn on the waterworks again. Twice in two days? I don't remember reading that the effects of altitude turn you into a quivering wreck!

I pulled myself together and focused on the day ahead. I forced down a bowl of porridge that tasted like cardboard and donned full winter gear (it was a frosty minus-five degrees outside). As we were standing outside, shivering, a porter passed with a pair of sandals on and no socks. The mountain people of Nepal are a hardy bunch.

We set off in the semi-light of 5.30am. The sun came up an hour later and soon we were down to base layers and light gloves. The weather gods where on our side and we were going to get to see all the mountains today, unhindered by the cloud that had screened them earlier in the week.

Gorak Shep Elevation: 5165m.

We trekked alongside the Khumbu glacier for four hours and reached a high point overlooking the village of Gorak Shep:

this would be our lunch stop and we would return here for our night's accommodation after, if everything went to plan, we had been to Base Camp.

Situated at 5165m above sea level, the village sits on a frozen lakebed covered in sand. It is not inhabited year-round and serves as a launch pad and base for climbers and trekkers heading to Everest. It was the original Everest Base Camp before the current Base Camp, which is closer to the Khumbu icefall, was founded. Gorak Shep is overlooked by the 5550m Kala Patthar, a mountain we had the option to climb tomorrow. I was hoping to do this, however my sole objective was to get to Everest Base Camp.

As we arrived at our accommodation, I was nearly knocked over by an onrushing trekker, bursting outside to be sick. This was not a good sign as we were readying for an early lunch. I opted for a tomato and noodle soup, thinking this would be the easiest thing to get down my neck. The dining room was not the cleanest we had been to and our group exchanged worried glances as we took our seats. My soup arrived with the thumb prints of the person who had brought it to me on the inside of the bowl. I tried to put this out of my mind, but I could only manage a few spoonfuls. Stuart didn't even touch his. He was looking a bit green – the result of a combination of the altitude and the unhygienic conditions. Our group ate lunch in silence. The friendly chats and jokes that had brought us closer together during this experience had evaporated in the thin air.

We were given the keys to our rooms and an opportunity to freshen up before the six-hour round trip to Everest Base Camp. I wanted to get going – partly because the goal was now tantalisingly close, but partly because I knew I didn't have much energy left in my tank, and the needle was dropping with every hour I spent at this altitude.

As I approached my room, another fellow hiker barged passed me and was sick in the communal toilet. Was this altitude sickness, or did he finish his soup?

The Khumbu glacier.

And – finally – on we went. I could see all the famous places I had read so much about: the Khumbu glacier; the Khumbu icefall; Nuptse and, poking her head out from among the other giants, Everest, the highest mountain in the world!

We saw three natural avalanches as we hiked. These were incredible to witness (from a safe distance). The thundering noise of the snow and ice coming down the mountains made an amazing soundtrack to our final few kilometres to Base Camp. Nitin joked that this was my birthday gift from the mountain Gods! Duncan got some amazing footage of one of the avalanches and sent it to us all later, a wonderful keepsake.

I was in a trance at this stage, I felt so determined to make it to Base Camp, even though every step seemed harder than the one before.

I remembered heading out of Namche, several days earlier, when Mingmau pulled me aside and told me I was setting too fast a pace. I had felt so strong at the start of the trek and had such confidence in my fitness. But when I turned around, I saw that our group had splintered into three. Mingmau decided to put Smita to the front of the group (she was called No.1), with Annette behind her (No.2), then Tina (No.3), followed by myself (No.4) and the rest of the group. The downside was I would need to stare at Tina's backside for the next four days!

Tina and I had developed a good friendship. She said I was like her little brother, constantly winding her up, but she took it in great spirits and we had some great laughs. She was selfless. When I got sunburn, she shared her amazing Paw Paw miracle ointment (I think this stuff literally cures anything). Tina had trouble with a recurring knee injury after day four and she hobbled all the way to Base Camp without a complaint. It was an amazing achievement and testimony to her mental strength and physical endurance.

Myself above Gorak Shep.

The only person I struggled to form a bond with was Smita. She was from Mumbai and the cultural difference between us prevented us from bonding, no matter how hard I tried. Duncan christened her 'Precious' as she had Mingmau carry her rucksack, put on her jacket and gloves and feed her water when required. I felt she treated Mingmau like a slave, but he seemed happy to look after her. Nitin explained that Smita was from a wealthy family and her behaviour would not have been out of the ordinary back home. I struggled with this: my humble beginnings are always with me and I treat others as I want to be treated.

We finally caught sight of our destination: Everest Base Camp was a mere 500m away. But it wasn't that easy: we had to drop down approximately 100m and then we'd have one last pull up to Base Camp, which sits at 5364m.

Phurba joked: did we want to just call it a day here and head back?

As we walked closer, the physical challenge of this trek was evident all around us. People were literally dropping like flies, others were being carried to Base Camp. Some people looked at this with derision, but I understood how it felt to be so close, with so little energy left. I would have crawled there on my hands and knees at this point.

As we ascended the last pull to Base Camp, Tina insisted that, as it was my birthday, I should go to the front: a selfless act from a wonderful human being. I was so tired that I resisted, but she pushed me to the front and at 2.30pm on October 13, 2019, my 40th birthday, my life's ambition was complete. I made it to Everest Base Camp.

I thought about the year I had spent recovering from my illness, mentally and physically, to keep my date with Everest. Tears were streaming down my face. Again!

We hugged and congratulated each other. Our group was so diverse in terms of age and fitness but all ten of us had made it.

Everest poking her head out behind me.

Tina produced a birthday card for me, which the entire group signed. It's the most precious keepsake, something I know I will keep forever. And Stuart had a miniature of Glenfiddich malt whisky, which he had brought all the way from Scotland. It was a humbling gesture.

When Phil and I first met on the Munros, we quickly found we had loads in common. We climbed five Munros on our first outing together. The fourth was my 100th in total, and No.182 for Phil, meaning he had another 100 to go to complete all 282 Munros. At the summit, I produced a hip flask filled with malt whisky and toasted our success. We finished that flask and the day's last Munro was tackled on wobbly legs. We christened our tandem walking group the 100 Dram Club that day. Over the subsequent years, various people have joined us on our walks and laughed when, at the summit, another expensive malt is produced.

Phurba enjoying Scotland's finest export.

Now the 100 Dram Club was continued at 5364m, albeit without one of its founding members. I took a small sip of the malt whisky, and it tasted amazing. Phurba and Mingmau enjoyed Scotland's finest export for the first time and enjoyed it greatly.

We queued in line for 20 minutes to have our photograph taken at a large rock that had been spray-painted: Everest Base Camp 5364m. My friend James Burns had been there 10 months previously and the sign wasn't there, but at least it was a good opportunity for a photo. When I climb mountains, I like to take a dramatic photo at the top of a trig point or cairn. That was my plan for today: to get on top of the rock and get a photo with the amazing, snow-capped peaks as a backdrop.

Made it!

As I got closer to the front of the line, I felt really cold. I stood in front of the rock and I barely had enough energy to stand, let alone climb the rock. I took out the Scottish Saltire flag Phil had used on his last Munro and I welled up again, full of pride and a sense of achievement; a normal guy like me, from humble beginnings, standing at Everest Base Camp!

The group at Everest Base Camp.

I took some time to wander around and dropped down as close as I could to the Khumbu Ice Fall. Base Camp was deserted at this time of year; it would have been good to see the tented village that pops up during the climbing season. Phurba said we would have been kept away from the climbers to ensure they didn't catch any colds or bugs before their Everest ascents, anyway. I kicked into the shale-like surface on the ground and an inch or two under the stone was ice. We were literally standing on a glacier. This had been another entry on my bucket list: to stand on a glacier.

Caroline and I had done this by going up the Jungrafrau Express train journey in Switzerland, the previous year. The glacier there was covered in snow. At Base Camp you could see the ice. Oh, and we had to walk for eight days to get there!

Scotland meets Base Camp.

I found another spray-painted rock a metre higher, at 5365m, and bumped into Josh and Mark, two Australian guys I had seen earlier on the trail. They were wearing Iron Man baseball caps and competed on the triathlon circuits in

Australia – two fit guys. I would say: "Hello Iron Men," and they called me Superman. We had these funny exchanges most days, without much more conversation than that. We exchanged high fives and congratulated each other on getting to Base Camp.

I asked Josh to take my photograph and he looked at me with a surprised expression on his face. I asked again, and again. Finally, I gestured with my phone to him.

The Khumbu icefall.

"Oh, you want your photograph taken?" he asked, before

obliging.

His friend Mark came from behind the rock with a can of Everest beer. I said: "That must be the best-tasting beer you've ever had." He gave me the same perplexed look Josh had given me. I had thought they were good guys, so why were they treating me like an idiot?

When I tried to repeat myself to Mark he acted like he finally got it: "Oh, you want a drink of my beer?" I waved them off and re-joined my group for the three-hour trek back to Gorak Shep.

Unbeknown to me at the time, I was really struggling with the effects of altitude. My lungs were frozen and I could barely speak, hence the incredulous looks from Mark and Josh. In my mind, I just felt tired and the words were coming out as normal. However, in reality all I was doing was opening my mouth and staring, like a fish.

I went from No.4 in the group to No.10 or, as we call it in Scotland, 'tail-end Charlie'. I felt my legs were moving fine, but I was going nowhere fast. Phurba had been propping up the rear for the past five days and he asked if I was okay. I said I was fine, just a bit cold and tired. As we were walking along a narrow ridge, he filmed me and then showed me the video. I was staggering around like a drunk. I couldn't believe it was me.

Phurba asked me later if I wanted to climb Kala Patthar for sunset. I said: "No chance." And that, he later told me, was when he knew I was suffering from altitude sickness. He remembered that I had said I would climb Kala Patthar at any cost, earlier in the trip.

Myself and the famous 'Way to Everest' sign.

Stuart and I kept each other motivated on the long walk back to Gorak Shep, but both of us were struggling badly now. We had full winter gear on and it was freezing. I was determined to get my photograph at the 'Way to Everest Base Camp' sign just outside Gorak Shep. Mingmau took my photo as the rest of the group staggered back to our accommodation. In my semi-conscious state, I forgot about how bad the teahouse was and both Stuart and I fell into our respective beds, utterly exhausted. We still had our down jackets and boots on and lay there groaning for an hour. I had never felt so tired in all my life. I had given everything I had to get to

Everest Base Camp.

We finally roused after an hour and had a wet wipe wash that took forever; even the simplest of tasks was an effort at this height. We staggered down for dinner at 7pm. The rest of the group were not in great shape, either. Celebrations were on hold for another day.

I opted for a vegetable spring roll, hoping that it would go down a lot easier than the ubiquitous rice or the putrid soup I had in the same place at lunch. I had barely eaten today and burned 3000 calories – no wonder I felt as bad as I did. My spring roll arrived and just looking at it made me feel sick. *Mind over matter, Paul, you can do this.* I cut the roll open to reveal a long pubic hair. Ordinarily, this wouldn't bother me. I would remove the offending item, complain profusely and get my meal for free. Not tonight. No matter how hard I tried to convince myself I needed the calories, I could not bring myself to eat.

Phurba congratulated us on our achievement and offered us the opportunity to climb Kala Patthar at 2.30am. I had decided on the way back from Base Camp that I wasn't going to do it. I had used up all the energy reserves I had getting back to Gorak Shep. The rest of the group felt the same, apart from Derek, the most senior member of the group. He wanted to tackle the climb.

We went to bed at 8.30pm. There was no Wi-Fi and I was aching to contact Caroline, to tell her I had made it to Base

Camp and to hear from her on my special birthday. The room was freezing all night long. I put on my Workwear & PPE pom-pom hat, but even fully clothed inside my sleeping bag, I was shivering.

***

My nightly ritual before bed was to filter half-a-litre of water, which I would try to drink during the night, to keep dehydration and altitude sickness at bay (despite knowing I would have to go to the toilet two or three times as a result). I was so exhausted I slept through to 4am and woke with the worst headache I have ever had. I could barely open my eyes, my mouth had stuck closed and I couldn't speak to let Stuart know of my situation. He told me later that he could hear me groaning and thought I was having a bad dream, when in fact I was trying to get his attention.

I felt like I was in severe trouble. Phurba had told us all about the symptoms and effects of altitude sickness and I was experiencing them all, but there was nothing I could do about it other than wait for Stuart to wake and get Phurba. I lay in my sleeping bag holding the key ring Caroline had bought me, hoping that if the worst happened at least she would know I was thinking of her. It seems crazy now, but at the time I believed I was dying.

Stuart finally woke at 5.30am and helped get me sitting upright in my sleeping bag. He suggested I get Phurba, but I could barely sit up, let alone walk down the steep stairs to the room he and Mingmau slept in. Thankfully, Stuart brought Phurba to the room.

I knew by the look on his face that my condition had indeed worsened. That, and the fact that he said: "Fuck me Paul, you look bad." It was not the encouragement I was expecting. Phurba took my readings: a resting heart rate of 112 and my oxygen levels had dropped down to a concerning 70%. This was right on the rescue level limit he had reminded us of every day. He told me to drink two litres of water and to find him at breakfast. I had to drop 200 metres urgently to reduce the effects of altitude sickness.

Today was going to be a 20km day and I could barely get dressed and brush my teeth! I went down to the dining hall and sat with my head in my hands, it felt as if it was in a vice. The group were concerned but while I appreciated their kind words, I just wanted to be left alone, to curl into a ball and die. I forced down a few spoonfuls of porridge. Later, they told me I was covered in food and slobbering like a two-year-old. I was oblivious to this.

Derek came back from his successful summit of Kala Patthar and sat next to me. I congratulated him and explained I was in a bad way, but I wanted to hear everything about his trip when I was better. He said he was so sorry I was feeling that way. I told him to leave me and to enjoy his achievement.

I later learned that Smita had spent a similarly rough night as she, too, suffered the effects of altitude. That morning,

Phurba decided she should be airlifted back to Kathmandu as her health was at serious risk.

There had been various reports of people feigning illness once reaching Base Camp and getting airlifted off. The excess on the insurance policy we had taken out was $750 for a helicopter rescue. The cost without insurance was $10,000, which would weed out the people who were really sick and those who wanted a free ride. Smita was in the former group and looked as bad as I felt. On reflection, she had been struggling with both the altitude and the endurance aspect of the trek and perhaps I should have been a bit more understanding of her tribulations. We met up again in Kathmandu and she was a different person, away from the demands of the trail and the beneficiary of a few days' rest.

A 'Khumbu taxi' coming in to land.

Phurba offered me a place on the helicopter as it would be six hours before we dropped the required 200 metres in altitude that would hopefully kickstart my recovery. We were retracing yesterday's route and today was going to be a day of ups and downs, followed by a steep drop later in the day. I was determined to walk back to Lukla. Phurba explained I could be back in the 30-degree sunshine of Kathmandu in three hours, sipping a beer, instead of struggling for the next six hours and having to walk to Lukla over the next three days.

It *did* sound appealing. However, it was not what I had come here to do. I felt my achievement would be tainted and it would appear premeditated – get to Base Camp and then take the easy way down. Also, it was $750. I had plenty of things I wanted to buy in Kathmandu.

Gorak Shep – Pangboche

Step by step, hour after hour, I found myself in the middle of the group, shuffling one foot in front of the other in silence. We reached Lobouche and I wasn't sure if I was going to pass out, be sick or defecate myself. I spoke to Phurba and he said this was a good sign: I could now feel something; prior to that I had just felt numb.

I staggered into a hut that was serving tea and forced down a Snickers bar, my first decent nutrition in two days. After that, as each minute passed, I started to feel better. I managed to get Wi-Fi and spoke to Caroline and my family by text. And I caught up with all my birthday wishes, which lifted my spirits.

A yak framed against the backdrop of a snow covered peak.

As we retraced our outward route, downhill for the majority of today's trek, I was feeling good. We reached our planned overnight stop at Pheriche, on the opposite side of the valley from our earlier two-night stop at Dingboche, around 2pm. I managed one third of my large portion of chow mein (no garlic) and we bumped into the 'Giggle Squad'. They were still in high spirits and the altitude had done nothing to stifle their infectious laughter.

Phurba asked how we were all feeling. Everybody seemed fine now. He asked if we wanted amend our plan and carry on to Pangboche for the night. There lay the promise of en suite rooms and a first shower for five days. The decision was unanimous and instant.

We dropped into a valley beside a river and pulled up over a high pass in the clouds. The temperature dropped and we didn't see anyone for hours. We were off the trail now. Most of us had developed head colds, myself included. As we sneezed in chorus, all the way to Pangboche, we realised why every vendor on the trail sold tissues.

Me arriving at Pheriche finally feeling normal again.

We could see our teahouse in the distance and reached it as darkness fell. I had an amazing shower and a cheese sandwich with chips. The troubles of the past day were behind me, I was feeling great again and my spirits were high. Stuart, Duncan, Derek and I stayed up later than usual and I managed to catch up on messages and spoke to Caroline. But I spared her the details of my ordeal over the previous 24 hours.

Pangboche – Namche

I awoke on Day 10 feeling great, aside from my head cold and Khumbu cough, and I would have taken that yesterday. The whole group were in good spirits – the atmosphere was more like it had been earlier in the trip, when we were always having a laugh together. The energy of the group had diminished at the highest point of our adventure, but it was getting stronger now.

We had a steep climb up to the village of Tengboche and I finally got to go into the famous Buddhist monastery also known as Dawa Choling Gompa. Most climbers of Everest and the surrounding high mountains visit here for a blessing from the monks before attempting their climb. It was deserted today. We had a wander around and went outside to enjoy the sun for a short while; the increase in temperature compared to our last few days was a tonic. We were still at 3800m (three times higher than the highest point in the UK) but we were returning to civilisation slowly and it felt great.

The monastery was built in 1916 and is the largest in the Khumbu region. It was levelled by an earthquake in 1934 and subsequently rebuilt, before being destroyed again in 1989, this time by fire. It was reconstructed once more by volunteers, with some overseas assistance.

Me outside the Tengboche Monastery.

While we were waiting for the rest of the group to come out of the monastery, a wild donkey approached Duncan, who was eating some roasted nuts. He gave the beast some and we had a new member of our group. No matter how hard Mingmau tried, he couldn't get the donkey to leave. He hit it on the backside with his trekking pole and it tried to head butt him. After all we'd come through over the past few days, surely we weren't going to be killed by a wild donkey. The creature started to hound Duncan for the remainder of his nuts. Stuart pointed out the donkey was getting rather excited and on closer inspection had the largest erection I had ever seen. This thing was like a baseball bat! We quickly mustered the rest of the group, grabbed our gear and left. Most people remember Tengboche for the famous monastery. We would remember it for the horny donkey.

We dropped into a warm, steep valley, where we enjoyed tea in the sun, overlooking the Dudh Kosi River, at 3250m. This was a moment to savour, and we were all now conscious that our trip-of-a-lifetime would be coming to an end soon.

Last view of Everest.

Our next objective would be to return to the bustling town of Namche. I was looking forward to getting there. It was a tough, steep climb of 600m in the afternoon – so much for the return route being easier! We passed through a small village and picked up some gifts for friends and family. The heat of the sun was amazing, it felt like a holiday now: we were under no pressure to get to Namche for a certain time; altitude sickness was no longer an issue; we had achieved our goal. It was time to enjoy ourselves.

The Hilary bridge. We had come so far from crossing it days ago and would be crossing it tomorrow.

Far in the distance, we could see the Hilary Bridge and the Everest View Hotel. What a difference a week makes – we were returning to Namche with smiles on our faces, looking forward to the familiarity of some Western comforts. The life of the trail continues all around us and we passed numerous porters carrying what seemed to me to be even heavier loads. Their Nepalese music was no longer an annoyance, but a pleasant and memorable soundtrack to our trip.

We reached Namche at 4.30pm. Once more, our teahouse was at the highest point of the village, but now that was a bonus, because we were heading downhill. We got the keys to our rooms, but decided to head out straight away. After being away for six days, the packed streets of Namche were an assault on the senses. Phurba told us every available bed in the village was taken and our porters had to sleep in tents outside the teahouse.

Arriving back at Namche a week after leaving!

I purchased a map detailing our route, which would be a great keepsake: one to show the grandkids! As I passed a hair salon, the gentleman outside asked if I wanted a haircut. I took my hat off to reveal my lack of hair, but he said he could shave it and give my face a shave as well. I didn't need to be asked twice. It had been 18 years since I visited a hair salon as I shave my head myself, every day. Now I settled into my comfortable chair, lay back and let the barber work his magic. I didn't know it at the time, but Mingmau, our guide, was sitting next to me in the salon, getting his head and face shaved. He later told me that I had nearly fallen asleep in the chair! I emerged from my trance-like state relaxed and refreshed and smelling better than I had done for a long time.

Phurba with his Workwear & PPE hat.

While the rest of the group continued their shopping, I decided to head back to the teahouse to catch a sneaky shower. As usual, Mingmau glided up the steep steps of Namche, but my breathlessness reminded me that we were still over 3000m above sea level. There was one person in front of me in the shower queue and despite this residence being a lot more luxurious than our previous seven teahouses, the shower was in an outside hut. When I came out, darkness had fallen, as had the temperature. I scampered back to my room to get some warm clothes on.

I had a cheese sandwich for dinner (my appetite had still not returned). I had burned another 2000 calories; goodness knows how much weight I had lost in the past week. I gave Phurba my Workwear and PPE pom-pom hat that I had promised him earlier in the trek. He put it on for a photo: never has our hat been worn by a stronger or more resilient model. I told him I was disappointed about how I had felt the day after Base Camp, as I had ambitions to climb some big mountains in the future and was now concerned about how I would cope at similar altitudes. He assured me I would have been fine and that I just needed a morning's rest, time we unfortunately didn't have on the trek. Had I been attempting to climb Everest, I would have got to Base Camp and rested for a week, before starting my rotation up and down the mountain to acclimatise. This made me feel better, but it did not dispel the doubts I have about my ability to complete a big climb at altitude. And knowing my personality, I may well end up putting those doubts to the test in the future.

We went to bed knowing that day 11 would be our final day of trekking and also our longest, with a lot of ascents and descents. It wasn't time to take our feet off the gas yet.

Namche – Lukla

Carry me back station. A great cause.

After another early rise – 5.30am this time – and more porridge, we left Namche at 6.30am. I picked another couple of gifts for family as we were leaving the village and had to run to catch up with the rest of the group. We reached the Carry Me Back station at the start of the village and each of us carried a small 1kg parcel of plastic and recyclable waste back to Lukla. It was easy to be a part of such a great project.

We dropped down the forest trail to the Hillary Bridge. The trail was much busier now and there was a stream of uphill trekkers passing us, the hope and expectation apparent in their faces. We must have looked like that on our way up, but now we just looked like a bunch of dirty, dishevelled hippies. At least we *felt* great.

Even freezers have to be carried by human power!

We reached the Hillary Bridge and I took an amazing photograph: the bridge appeared to go on forever and the image caught the glare of the morning sun perfectly. We crossed several suspension bridges and had to wait at most of them for the yak trains to cross. We almost got caught when a yak train came behind us. We ran across the bouncing bridge, fearful of catching the horns of a yak in our backsides.

We finally reached Phurba's teahouse five hours after setting off, all a bit tired by the morning's trek. A lunch of fried rice was enjoyed, perhaps too much as I wasn't in the mood to get back on the trail. We chatted with a group of three English folk who said the remainder of the journey to Lukla was a steep, uphill three-hour trek. Nothing comes easy in the Khumbu valley.

Crossing the Hilary suspension bridge on our way back.

We said our goodbyes to Phurba's family, the ladies in our group fussing over his new-born son. It's amazing what babies can do to lighten the mood and bring smiles to people's faces. Phurba confirmed that the afternoon's trek would be difficult, but the payback was hefty: we had the luxury of a hotel with clean rooms, free Wi-Fi, warm en-suite showers, flushable toilets and free gadget charging waiting for us in Lukla. Our hotel would be close to the airport, for an early-morning flight back to Rammechap.

Stuart, Tina, Annette and I discussed the possibility of taking a helicopter directly from Lukla to Kathmandu, rather than the flight to Rammechap followed by the long, hot bus journey. I really wanted to experience the flight out of Lukla, having missed it on the way up, and I didn't want a repeat of the hours spent waiting for the helicopter on the way up. However, Phurba assured us that the helicopter would be ready on our arrival in Lukla, and our decision was made. It would be the direct route to Kathmandu for us.

After a long, tough climb, we finally arrived in Lukla at 5pm and (you guessed it) our hotel was at the furthermost point of the town. For the first time on the trip I could feel some blistering on my heels. Rather than attend to it, I just kept walking. I had been through enough and I just wanted to get to the hotel.

Lukla is situated 2860m above sea level, double the elevation of the highest point in Scotland (Ben Nevis) and it was the lowest point on our trek. As we walked through the bustling small town, we passed an Irish bar and, amazingly, a Scottish bar. There was, however, no time to enjoy a nice pint of Tennents lager – our goal was a warm shower in the Buddha Lodge. We passed the famous airport and the airstrip was as terrifying as it had looked online. I saw four helicopters parked up for the evening and I was looking forward to getting back the bustle and heat of Kathmandu.

The Scottish pub in Lukla.

The Buddha Lodge was advertised as 'luxurious' so when we reached our accommodation at 5.45pm, I presumed we had arrived at the wrong place. This was *Nepalese* luxury and everything is relative. The rooms were dirty and cold, but at least we could charge our gadgets for free. With the temperature dropping, the dirty sleeping bags were brought back out for another night. Now for the long awaited, luxurious warm shower.

I had learned from the many unpredictable shower experiences I had survived and I suspected the hot water may be limited or, at times, scalding. My established technique was this: I would lather up with shower gel and due to the lack of hot water and sometimes scalding water I would use a loofer to rinse the soap off. Despite the outward appearance of a modern, en-suite shower, I decided to stick to the plan. After lathering all over, I turned the shower on and it was ice cold! I couldn't believe it! I stood there trying to muster up the mental strength to stand under the water, but I just couldn't do it.

I walked out into the corridor of the hotel and shouted on Duncan, hoping to use his shower. However, I got more attention than I intended and several people emerged from their rooms to see an emaciated, white Scotsman covered in soap, having a mini meltdown. I quickly established that none of the rooms had any hot water left. I went back inside, got the down jacket back out and had my final wet-wipe shower. As funny as it seems now, at the time it almost tipped me over the edge.

After a quick change, it was time for our farewell dinner in the hotel's restaurant. This would give us the opportunity to spend some time with the porters who had carried our bags every day. Mingmau would wake us every morning we were on the trail and ensure our duffle bags were packed and ready to go. The porters would come and collect them and that would be the only time we would see them. They would arrive at our next stop three or four hours ahead of us, despite the porters carrying four or five times the weight we were carrying. They were absolute machines.

We were introduced to the five porters, who, along with Phurba and Mingmau, gave us a table of 17 for this last supper. The trekkers had agreed that we would be paying the bill and we ensured the porters had plenty of beer, despite the fact that they would have been asked for ID before they got inside a pub back home. One of them weighed 41kg but carried upwards of 30kg each day. We had a good laugh with the porters and despite the language difficulties between us, they had a great night, smiling and enjoying our company.

As a group we had decided to give 10% of our trip as a tip to the guides and porters. This equated to $140 per person. As the eldest of the group, Derek gathered all the money and gave a lovely speech of thanks to Phurba, Mingmau and the porters for all their efforts in helping get us to Everest Base Camp. We couldn't have done it without them.

Phurba took Derek away for a private chat and it turned out they had a foolproof system of dividing up the tips. Phurba gave each of the group a bundle of cash that was to go to each of the porters and guides. Mine was to go to Mingmau and I was delighted. The two of us had formed a real bond and I had a huge amount of respect for him. The porters and guides seemed grateful for their gifts. Then the music came on and the party got into full swing. The porters and guides were on the dance floor, along with the other diners. It was great to see them enjoying themselves after working so hard for the past 11 days. However, our group were too tired to dance and sat at the table enjoying a few Sherpa beers.

We headed to bed around 10pm, leaving Phurba, Mingmau and the porters on the dance floor. This was one of our latest nights – it hadn't been a holiday for partying. Phurba said we would have to be up at 6.30am for our helicopter flight. The other members of the group were to get up an hour earlier to wait for their flight back to Rammechap.

Lukla – Kathmandu

Mingmau chapped our door at 5.30am precisely with his usual cheery, "Good morning!" He clearly hadn't received the memo. In the politest way we could at such an hour, Stuart and I informed him that we had booked the helicopter and would be claiming our extra hour in bed.

By the time we got there, the restaurant was all but deserted, a lot quieter than we were here the night before. I gulped down a quick omelette and a cup of tea before Phurba said it was time to go. Stuart and I waited for Annette and Tina, outside the hotel. I saw a stray dog tending to her pups and had a pang of homesickness; I couldn't wait to get back to see Caroline and my two dogs.

We had been advised to add an extra day onto our holiday as the flights out of Lukla are notoriously temperamental. I had heard about people being stuck in Lukla for days. If we became stranded, our trekking company would put on a 4 x 4 to take us the 16 hours back to Kathmandu. But as the sun came up, I could see it was a cloud free day and I was positive about our chances of making it out on time.

*Finally getting to see Lukla airport after
missing out on our outward journey.*

We passed the airport, which has tens of people standing watching flights leave every morning. I wondered if they watched on the off chance that the plane never made it off the end of the runway. Our departure point was not the airport though. We followed Phurba around every nook and cranny of Lukla, passing a street market where they were cutting fresh meat on the ground, ready to be carried for days up the trail without refrigeration. I was glad I had stuck to a vegetarian diet.

Then we were in someone's garden, which had a few steps down into a large flat field. This was to be our helicopter strip. The porters carried our bags, their final job for us. They would get two days' rest now, before heading back up the trail for the next 11 days. That schedule would repeat for the rest of the season: a tough way to make a living. There were stray dogs running around the landing strip. It was organised chaos, but by now I had become accustomed to the pace and unique flavour of life in Nepal. In that context, feral dogs circling a makeshift helicopter pad at the back of someone's garden seemed like the most natural thing in the world.

Another day, another helicopter.

Several helicopters landed and quickly took off for rescue missions: the Khumbu taxis, as Mingmau called them. I had a feeling we had been here before. What was Nepalese for déjà vu?

Phurba said there would be only be five spaces for the first flight, as the first two were taken up by a German climber and his partner. Stuart selflessly said Tina, Annette and I should board this helicopter and he would catch us up. We said a quick goodbye to Phurba and Mingmau and boarded the chopper, with me riding shotgun again.

I put the headphones on and readied for takeoff. I'm no expert on air traffic control, but our pilot was having difficulty getting permission for takeoff. Every time he went to speak, someone else spoke over him. He was getting very frustrated and started to swear into his mic. This went on for about 15 minutes and then he appeared to make a unilateral decision to take off.

I had visions of our helicopter crashing into one above us, as had almost happened at the start of our trip. I exchanged looks with our frustrated pilot. Mine: 'I don't think this is a good idea'. His: 'Okay then, suit yourself, I'll wait'.

Once we were up in the air, the flight back was very relaxing. We saw the plane carrying the rest of our group take off and take a different route, through the valleys, as we went directly over the mountains. I could pick out the trails and small villages along the journey. Not so long ago, this would be the trekking route from Kathmandu to Lukla. It would take around three days, instead of an hour's helicopter flight. We approached the high-rise buildings of Kathmandu and I could see it was a scorching hot day, despite being early morning.

We touched down at the far side of Kathmandu airport. As I got off the flight, an official approached and in broken English told me there was an ambulance waiting for me at the exit. I was confused. Would my experience of altitude sickness at Base Camp four days ago require me to go to hospital? We had heard that Smita, who left us at Gorak Shep by helicopter, had spent three days in hospital. I just wanted to get back to my hotel for a shower.

A brand-new van was waiting to transport us across the airport. The smell of the air freshener and leather seats were an assault on our senses. I couldn't get my head around how good the van smelled. I wondered if the driver thought the same about us? We got off the mini-bus and two ambulancemen approached me, saying they were taking me to hospital. As I asked why this was necessary, they grabbed me by each arm and started to usher me toward the ambulance. I looked around at Tina and Annette, and could see the German man putting his hand up. I hadn't noticed on the chopper, but he looked seriously ill. I helped him with his bag and he and his partner were taken away in the ambulance. At the time it seemed like an amusing case of mistaken identity, but it also stood as a reminder of how my own trip could easily have ended.

Tina, Annette and I were let out of a side gate and were met by a representative from Himalayan Wonders, our tour company. He took us to our taxi, where we would wait for Stuart. After 11 days on the trail, it was lovely to stand in the 30-degree heat, watching the hustle and bustle of life around Kathmandu airport. Stuart arrived, minus his duffle bag and all his worldly possessions. His helicopter had reached its weight capacity before take off and they had to leave his bag on the strip at Lukla. He had been promised he would be reunited with it, but he was clearly worried.

The mid-morning taxi journey from Kathmandu airport to our hotel in Thamel was as exhilarating as I remembered it. Just 13 days had passed since we had made the opposite journey, but it seemed like a lifetime ago. We had shared a unique experience and we were changed.

As we approached our hotel, we could see Smita sitting on the breakfast balcony. She came over and gave us a warm greeting. She looked dramatically better than she had when we left her at Gorak Shep. She was wearing nice clothes, and she smelled great. Goodness knows what she thought of us.

Smita joined us for breakfast: fresh toast, a chef-cooked omelette, yoghurts, cakes and tea. We gorged ourselves on the delicious, fresh food. It had been a long time since we had tasted anything like this.

We had left a bag of clean clothes and toiletries at the hotel before heading off on the trek. I quickly found mine amongst the hundreds that were piled high in the basement. However, it was still early, and in my considerable experience, a hotel room tends to be ready by mid-afternoon, regardless of the time you arrive. But after a few phone calls from the receptionist to housekeeping, we were told our room was ready. I could not have been happier.

Stuart got the key and we opened the door to a freshly cleaned room. Never has the smell of bleach been so alluring. There was an en suite, flushable toilet; a toilet roll on a holder, rather than in our bags; air conditioning and clean warm beds. I've stayed in every kind of place on my travels, from five-star resorts (with Caroline) to bunkhouses and hostels (during my hillwalking trips) but I had never been more appreciative of my accommodation – our three-star hotel felt like seven-star luxury compared to some of the places we had stayed in since we were last in Kathmandu.

I lay on the bed, appreciating the luxuries we now had, and I'm unashamed to say I sat on the toilet pan for longer than necessary, enjoying the feeling of clean porcelain beneath me, after hovering over disgusting toilets for the past 11 days. I had a long shower while Stuart was on the telephone to the trekking company, trying to locate his bag. We chilled for a few hours, catching up with social media and messages from back home. I finally felt like we were on a proper holiday, with the hardships and worries of the trek behind us.

Stuart and I went back to our favourite place, the Road House Café, and enjoyed pizzas, fries and coke, more of the things we had missed. It was a delicious lunch enjoyed in the sunshine.

We had a wander around the shops and stumbled across an art gallery. Derek had told me he had found a beautiful painting on our first day in Namche and had purchased it on the promise he would collect it on our way back. I was keen to see it, but it was securely wrapped and the first time I saw it was when he sent me a photograph, after we were home. I'm not a great lover of art, but I thought a nice painting would be a great keepsake from my trip. As I walked into the gallery, one painting jumped off the wall at me. I spoke to the owner of the gallery and he said he wanted $600 for it. After the razor-and-sun cream affair in Namche, I decided to tell the gallery owner I would come back, giving me the opportunity to consider my negotiation strategy in the meantime. There are literally hundreds of art galleries in Kathmandu and it felt like Stuart and I went to all of them, but I couldn't get that painting out of my mind: prayer flags and a herd of yaks, set against the majestic backdrop of Everest and her sister peaks. Memories of my journey to Base Camp, captured forever.

Throughout the trek and our time in Nepal every structure was covered in prayer flags, including the suspension bridges. They are bright and are coloured, from right to left, blue, white, red, green and yellow. Blue represents the sky, white the air, red fire, green water and yellow symbolises earth. I picked up some flags and my sister Karen put them inside a beautiful frame, along with my certificate from Himalayan Wonders, documentary evidence that I had completed the trek.

We got back to the hotel just as those of the group who had taken the plane and bus arrived, looking a bit hot and bothered from the six-hour bus ride in the baking sun. Derek and Simon had wisely booked into a luxurious five-star hotel on the other side of Kathmandu and we agreed to meet up later (the rest of the group were staying in the same hotel as Stuart and I).

The painting I finally bought.

Stuart and I continued exploring the city and finally headed back to the hotel in the late afternoon. As we entered the hotel, Duncan called us from the balcony of the cafe across the road. He had been enjoying cocktails with Nitin, Annette and Tina all afternoon. We sat with them for a few hours, enjoying each other's company. When we returned to the hotel, Stuart's bag was waiting for him. He was as happy as he was relieved.

We had a quick shower and headed out for our farewell dinner, put on by Himalayan Wonders and hosted by Raine.

We teamed up with another group and enjoyed a lovely dinner together. I had a beer aptly named Everest. It had been Simon's birthday the day before and Derek had arranged for a cake to be presented to him in the restaurant. Simon was over the moon and the whole restaurant sang *Happy Birthday* to him. We saw the Giggle Squad for the last time, still smiling and entertaining us with their infectious laughs.

After dinner, we walked around the busy streets of Thamel, before settling into a pub. I ordered a Glenfiddich malt whisky and the rest of the group enjoyed cocktails. Most of the pubs close early in Kathmandu compared to the UK. We said our goodbyes to Simon and Derek as they took a taxi to their hotel. The rest of us retired to our rooms around midnight.

I was desperate to see the best of Kathmandu before heading home and I arranged with Himalayan Wonders to organise a personalised tour of the city. Stuart, Duncan, Annette and Tina would join me on our last day together.

Sacred Memories

I had arranged a 9.30am start for our bespoke, farewell tour of Kathmandu – decadent, compared with our usual pre-dawn alarm calls during the trek. Maybe that routine was to blame for Stuart and I waking up at 6.30am. We met the others for breakfast and our guide for the day collected us from our hotel.

Stupa in the monkey temple.

Our bus weaved its way through the busy streets of Kathmandu. After climbing mountains, I think exploring cities is my favourite past time. We arrived at our first stop, Swayambbhunath Stupa – otherwise known as the Monkey Temple, due to the monkeys wandering around the sacred site. The stupa sits 3km outside Kathmandu, with amazing views over the city, and was built in the 13th century. It is one of the holiest and oldest Buddhist sites in Nepal.

Monkeys in the famous monkey temple.

As we explored the holy site, taking pictures and enjoying the warm sunshine, I spun the large prayer wheel. I wasn't asking for luck to make it to Base Camp anymore; this time my prayer was one of thanks, for making it there and back safely. Through all of this, Tina waited in the bus. I thought she was joking when she first claimed a lifelong fear of monkeys, but as my attempts to convince her to enter the stupa failed repeatedly, I realised that her phobia was real.

Our next stop was the Pashupatinath Hindu Temple, located on the Bagmati River on the eastern outskirts of Nepal. This site attracts hundreds of elderly followers of Hinduism, who arrive here hoping to meet death and be cremated in the sacred river, which flows into the holy river, the Ganges. I have been to India, and I've seen television programmes about the ashes of the dead being washed into the Ganges.

Prayer wheels.

As non-Hindus, we could only access certain areas of the sacred site. As our guide led us over to the river, we passed numerous monkeys and stray dogs, vying for food from tourists and locals alike. We saw holy men, which we were told are called Sadhus. They are wandering, ascetic yogis, seeking liberation from the cycle of death and rebirth by meditating. Their faces and bodies are painted yellow: quite a sight.

Monument in the Monkey temple.

As we passed close to the river, I could see two men sweeping burning ashes into the water. It didn't dawn on me then, but this was clearly the aftermath of a cremation. Across from us we could see a dead body sitting on the steps, an elderly woman who was next in line for cremation. It felt wrong to watch it, but our guide assured us it was perfectly natural and encouraged us to stay where we were and observe.

Ashes getting swept into the Bagmati River.

The family had gathered around the woman and cleaned her with water from the river. Some of them were smartly dressed, others wore shorts with no top. Our guide explained that cremation had to take place within 24 hours of death. Family members would get a phone call and drop everything to get to the temple. The woman was then carried over to a concrete bed. We respectfully walked along side, observing from the opposite bank. It felt surreal. The family prayed over the body and performed a short ceremony before a firelighter was placed in the woman's mouth. The flames quickly took hold and a wooden block was built around the woman, to keep the fire going. A few hours later, her ashes would be swept into the Bagmati River.

Our guide told us that a few hundred metres down river, locals would scour the riverbed for jewellery from the dead bodies. Further still downstream, women can be seen washing their clothing and bedding in the river, as the fats from the burning bodies form a residue that aids the removal of dirt[2].

The whole experience was fascinating and traumatic in equal measure, and ultimately humbling. As we were walking out, a pickup truck was reversing at great speed. I noticed it was about to hit a lame stray dog. I stood in the way of the vehicle and managed to get the dog to safety. The driver was not pleased and when I looked in the back of his truck I understood why: he had the next batch of dead, wrapped in cloth, ready for cremation. The five of us walked back to the bus in silent reflection.

Our final stop for the day was the Boudhanath Stupa. Located 11km outside of the centre of Kathmandu, this is one of the largest Buddhist stupas in the world. It was built in the 14th century and sits on a giant dome, with a Buddhist tower on top of it. It is an amazing sight, surrounded by a narrow square housing shops and restaurants.

[2] Legend has it that this was how soap was invented. In Roman times, women washed clothes in the River Tiber at the foot of Sappo Hill, a site of animal sacrifice. The animal fats in the river would form a clay-like substance.

We walked around the stupa, enjoying each other's company in the sunshine and knowing our trip of a lifetime was nearing an end. We ate lunch in a top floor restaurant with the views over the stupa. Duncan made a paper aeroplane and said he would be able to fly it over the square; it barely made it three feet and landed on the roof of the restaurant. I was going to miss his infectious personality.

Boudhanath Stupa.

As we walked around the square, our guide took us into a place where Mandala (literally 'circle') paintings were made. The Buddhists paint such designs to focus attention and they are used as spiritual guidance tools. Some of the paintings we saw would have taken years to complete, with the creator working 12 hours per day. I would have liked to purchase one, but I couldn't find one that met with my taste. And I had my heart set on the painting back in Kathmandu.

Backstreets of Thamel.

We got back to the hotel around 3pm. Back in the day, when I used to go to the football, at the end of the trip the bus convener would pass a hat around for a tip for the driver. It amused me (if nobody else) to do the same now, for our guide and driver. When we got to the hotel I passed the hat to the tour guide, encouraging him to take the money. He took the money out – and took my hat, for good measure. I had to chase after him and was able to convince him that he could keep the money, but return the hat.

Stuart, Duncan and I went for some last-minute shopping. In Namche, we had seen a large poster that showed our route from Lukla to Base Camp. Nitin wanted to buy it and I convinced him we would get it in Kathmandu, to save us carrying it all the way back to Lukla. Well, here we were and the pressure was on, but we must have tried 20 shops and none of them had a poster like we had seen in Namche.

We met Annette, Tina, Duncan and Nitin in the balcony bar across from the hotel and agreed to have dinner together, after a quick wash and change. However, by the time we got out, neither Stuart nor I could remember the name of the restaurant and we found ourselves wandering the streets, hoping to stumble into our friends. We finally caught up with them in an Indian restaurant just as they were finishing their meals. Nitin said he would order for me: not spicy and no garlic. This was met with confusion by the waiter, but Nitin made sure the instructions were followed. I enjoyed a lovely meal, washed down with an Everest beer. There was a band playing soothing Nepalese music, a fitting soundtrack with which to end to our trip.

Nitin had a good grasp of Nepalese and he agreed to come to the art gallery after dinner to negotiate the purchase of the painting I had seen the day before. I told him the gallery were looking for $600 and I was willing to pay $400. He said he would get it for $200. The owner remembered me and I introduced him to Nitin. As the discussion began, the owner called the artist to broker a deal. After 15 minutes of tense negotiating, Nitin said, "Let's go, they want too much money for the painting."

My first Everest beer.

"Hold on," I told him. "I'm willing to pay $400 and I really want it."

This was all part of the charade, but not something I was used to. We settled on the bargain price of $300. I was over the moon and I hoped that Caroline would feel the same when she saw it. It was an imposing piece: 6 feet wide and 4 feet tall.

I was keen for the gallery owner to post it to me, but Nitin insisted I take it home, just in case I had issues with customs further down the road. The gallery owner took it out of the frame and carefully rolled the painting up with protective paper and handed the four-feet tall roll to me. All I had to do was get it back to Scotland without damaging it or leaving it on the plane.

We slowly walked back to the hotel knowing our holiday of a lifetime was almost over. Stuart, Duncan and I would be getting picked up for the airport at 5am.

We said our goodbyes to Annette, Tina and Nitin, three remarkable people I hope to meet again someday. We set up a group chat for our entire group on WhatsApp and agreed to keep in touch; we had created a remarkable bond that words cannot describe. In two weeks, we had gone from complete strangers to friends for life.

Stuart and I packed our bags for one last time. That, at least, was something I wouldn't miss. For a while, at least.

Leaving Nepal

As our 5am taxi weaved its way through the streets of Kathmandu, the city was waking up to another day. By the time it was over, we would have left Nepal behind us.

We reached the busy airport and I managed to get my painting through customs without any issue. Due to our early start we decided to get breakfast at the airport, all we could buy was Pringles and Snickers bars: final guilty pleasures before returning to normality. In the business of the airport Stuart and I lost Duncan, but we managed to catch him briefly before his flight took off. He had been a great member of our group, likeable and funny. I'm certain our paths will cross in the future.

Our flight left Kathmandu on time. Stuart and I had a last gaze at the high peaks of Himalaya. We landed for our connecting flight in Dubai and had a few hours to kill. It felt crazy to be wandering around the luxurious, modern airport after all we had experienced in Nepal. I wondered if people would know by looking at us where we had been and what we had been through, as they were queuing for their gifts in duty free. They were probably oblivious, but I knew something had changed in me, and life would be slightly different when I got home.

Stuart spotted a Hard Rock Cafe a few hundred metres away. I begged him to go inside for food – I was craving a burger, having not eaten meat for the past 16 days. He tried to convince me it may not be a great idea as we had an eight-hour flight back to Glasgow ahead of us. I told Stuart that we would let the waiter decide. We had 50 minutes until our flight took off. If we could get a table and food within 25 minutes, we would go for it. "No problem" said the waiter.

I just had time to pick up some perfume for Caroline as our food was being prepared. And a burger has never tasted better. We were like cavemen gulping them down.

Our flight was full of Scottish folk coming back from the midterm school break, having enjoyed the best Dubai had to offer. I made a promise to bring Caroline to Dubai next year for her 40th birthday. She would love it here.

We finally arrived back in Glasgow late on Saturday night. Every time Caroline and I returned to this airport after a holiday, we'd always make the same joke about who would be waiting for us by the monitor showing the incoming flights in the arrivals lounge. The punchline was, there never was anyone. Until now.

I got my bags from the carousel and as I walked through arrivals, tired and disorientated, someone jumped on my back. I was so happy to see Caroline after such a long time apart, it was a wonderful surprise. As was the sight, as I opened the boot of her car to put my bags in, of our dog, Islay, who was as happy to see me as I was her. It was good to be home.

Caroline dropped me at my Dad's house, where I had left my car 16 days and one lifetime ago. My Dad gave me my birthday card and I hope he didn't mind that all I wanted to do was get home. I dropped Stuart off and finally got home at 10,30pm, after 22 hours of travelling.

I wanted to spend the whole of the next day in bed, knowing I was straight back to work on Monday. However, Caroline woke me early with all my birthday presents. With everything that had happened, I had forgotten that my 40th birthday had passed while I was away. Caroline told me we were going to see my sister Karen's new house. I barely had the energy to argue, and it was good to catch up with my Mum, Karen and Stephen, but I was glad to get back to some home comforts.

And that was it. Fourteen months in the making. A lifetime's ambition. Months of training and dieting, good health and bad. And now it was all over.

I don't think the achievement of getting to Everest Base Camp has sunk in as I write this. I had wanted this so desperately for so long, and after achieving my goal I found myself left with mixed emotions. We literally hadn't stopped for 16 incredible days and now I was able to reflect.

I was so happy to get back to my wonderful life in Scotland. I appreciate everything I have after my experiences in Nepal. I missed my wife and dogs greatly and I am so grateful to Caroline for allowing me to achieve my dream, despite her own anxieties about my trip.

Now what?

For once, I am not sure. I lost 3kg on the trek, taking me down to a skinny 62kg. All the muscle I had built has been burned off. I need to get some weight and muscle back on. I only have 31 Munros left to complete all 282, which has been an almost obsessive journey across 11 years. That is my immediate challenge.

The trip to Nepal has opened my eyes to a lot of future expeditions. But they are for another day.

EPILOGUE

It took some time for normal life to resume after my trip to Everest Base Camp. It was great to spend time with Caroline and to share all the stories of my adventures with her. The dogs were so happy to spend time with me.

The weekend after I got back, we had a small gathering of family and friends in Killin to belatedly celebrate my 40th birthday. Everyone was desperate to hear my stories, but I felt a sense of frustration trying to explain what it was like on the trek. It was unlike anything I or any of my friends and family had ever experienced.

Since returning, my pace of life had slowed down dramatically, and I felt a sense of calmness I had never had. I had always been striving for something and never satisfied. I no longer felt that way.

Stuart, too, was struggling to get back to normality. Friends and family told me I was being distant, but I was happy and content. Life felt amazing.

I climbed two Munros at Killin two weeks after returning and my fitness was still good; it was great to get back amongst the mountains, while knowing I could have a good feed and a warm shower at the end of the day.

As time passed, I would wake up during the night, sweating, after dreaming I was back in Namche, Phortse and Dingboche. It was if I was trying to make sense of what had happened, and I hadn't quite come to terms with it yet. A friend, Jim Hughes, had been to Nepal four times doing the Everest and Annapurna Base Camp treks and said I would be desperate to go back. I never admitted it to anyone, but I had no intentions of going back. At this stage, the bad memories heavily outweighed the good.

Two weeks before Christmas and with work quietening down, I spontaneously decided on a last-minute trip to Mexico with Caroline for some much-needed rest and relaxation. Since I had got back from Everest Base Camp, work had been crazy busy, and every weekend was spent on the mountains. This was time to reflect and recharge the batteries. And in this environment, with no stress or distraction, the hardship of the trip drifted to the back of my mind and I could only remember the positive aspects.

My every waking hour is now spent daydreaming of going back to Nepal. Stuart, Phil and I and hopefully some, if not all, of the group aim to go back, perhaps to the Annapurna or even to climb a mountain in Nepal over the next few years.

EQUIPMENT

I opted for comfort over weight on the trek. We were limited to 10kgs in our duffle bags, primarily for the flight to Lukla. There was no greater feeling than putting a nice, clean top and clean underwear on most nights. We managed to clean some clothes in a laundrette in Namche, but outwith that there was no opportunity for laundry on the trail. We struggled to get our towels dried some days.

Below is a list of the clothing and kit I took. Bear in mind we went in early October:

- Scarpa hillwalking 2 season leather boots x 1

- La Sportiva Helios Lightweight running shoes for wearing at night on the trek, travelling and for wearing in Kathmandu

- Flip flops for using in and before and after showers

- Merino wool underwear x 6. I prefer the brand Icebreaker

- Merino wool socks x 8 (6 lightweight, 2 midweight). I prefer the brand Bridgedale

- Baselayer tops, long sleeved with zip necks x 6. I had Rab, Montane, Berghaus and Mountain Equipment brands. Most outdoor brands have their own version. Some of the group preferred short sleeved t-shirts, all moisture wicking. I prefer long sleeved to protect my arms from the sun.

- Walking trousers x 2 (1 light pair and a heavier soft shell pair) both Mountain Equipment. I had the lightweight ones on up until Lobuche, but was glad of the heavier pair when it got colder

- Shorts x 1 (I took a pair of Mountain Equipment which were great for wearing in the heat of Kathmandu)

- Midlayer hooded full zip tops x 3 (I travelled with one on, left one in Kathmandu for my return journey and wore another on the trail. I had these on most days)

- Buffs x 3

- Baseball caps x 3 (I had 2 x North Face breathable caps and a Mountain Equipment shell cap)

- Warm hats x 3 (1 x Mountain Equipment 1 x Montane and a Workwear & PPE Pom Pom hat that I gave to Phurba)

- Gloves x 3 pairs (lightweight Mountain Equipment x1, heavier Rab leather gloves x 1 and a pair of warm Montane mittens which I wore on the day of Base Camp)

- Sunglasses

- Three-layer waterproof jacket (Mountain Equipment) I only wore this once on the way back from Base Camp, when I got really cold. It would have been a necessity if it had rained; thankfully, we never got caught in the rain once

- Three layer waterproof trousers (Berghaus) I never wore these

- Winter down jacket (Rab). I only wore this once on the trail, the morning of Base Camp. I should have taken it to Base Camp, but foolishly left it in Gorak Shep. I had it on every day after Namche, mostly in the rooms of the teahouses or when having a wet wipe shower. A great piece of kit

- Sleeping bag to -15. We brought a Rab version, which was great. I found it a bit too hot during the first few days of the trek, but it was a necessity for every night after Namche

- Osprey 48 litre day rucksack. It may have been too big, but I've used this is rucksack for climbing Munros for four years and I was comfortable with the weight, fit and the pockets. A 35-40 litre sack would have sufficed as you don't need to carry much on the trail. I preferred having everything I thought I might need, rather than not having it

- Stormtech 140 litre duffle bag. I struggled to get all my gear into my original North Face 110 litre duffle bag and had to purchase the Stormtech one the day before I left

- Dry bags x 4. I had 4 of various sizes. 1 for clean tops and underwear, 1 for clean trousers, mid layers hats and buffs, 1 for dirty clothing and a small one for toiletries

- Osprey 2 litre water bladder (I only ran out of water once. Bottled water is easily purchased on the trail, literally every 500m from Lukla to Namche and at teahouses for the rest of the trail)

- Toilet roll. This was readily available on the trail and due to my high-carbohydrate diet, I only used 3 rolls over the entire trail. However, I always made sure I had a full roll in my day sack and a full roll in my duffle bag

- Money belt. I wore this around Kathmandu and kept my cash and visas safe. In retrospect it is a very safe city, but I felt secure knowing it would be difficult to be a victim of a pickpocket while having this around my waist. On the trail I kept it in my rucksack

- Waterproof zip lock bags for storing medication and toilet roll

- Hikers first aid kit

- Grayl water purifying water press (this was the best piece of kit I took, highly recommended)

- Garmin Fenix 5 watch to record my route and statistics. Tina called me Statman as the group were always asking me for the daily readings

- Charger for the above

- Phone charger

- Battery pack (I resisted using this until later in the trek when power was a bit more erratic. When you charge your phones and devices, you have to leave them behind the counter, so you can't charge them in your room. The power pack enabled me to charge my watch and phone during the night)

- Book for night reading. I only read this on the plane and back in Kathmandu. We were so tired every night it was straight to bed after dinner

- Journal and pen (for writing this book)

- Microfibre bath towel. This was great as it dried quickly most days

TOILETRIES AND MEDICATION

- Toothbrush
- Toothpaste
- Razor
- Shaving foam
- 48-hour roll-in deodorant
- Paracetomol
- Diamox altitude sickness tablets. I purchased these online and they cost around £20 for 2 weeks' worth
- Vitamins
- Bite cream
- Wet wipes 2 large packets
- Chlorine tablet (I didn't use these but shared them around the group)
- Travel sickness tablets (I took one on the bus to Rammechap and it did the trick)
- Diarrhoea tablets (thankfully I didn't need to use these but they would have been a life saver if I had a bad stomach)

- Alcohol hand gel (vital for hygiene as there are very few places with running water after Namche)

- Mini Shower Gel x 2

- Loofer for washing (it was nice to have a home comfort when washing)

- Active root electrolytes. I took 20 pouches of these suitable for 500ml of water

COST OF TRIP (as of October 2019)

- The cost of the flight (Glasgow to Dubai with Emirates; Dubai to Kathmandu) was £900

- The cost of the hike including 2 nights in Kathmandu, 11 nights on the trail, 3 meals per day and 1 hot drink per meal, the flight to Lukla and back, guides and porters, a celebratory meal and drinks back in Kathmandu and airport transfers was $1395 US dollars.

- The flight to Lukla was included in the trip, but we had to pay $250 to get the helicopter from Rammechap to Surke. We could have waited until the next day with no extra cost. Relly did this, but as a result lost a day, during which we did an acclimatisation hike. He probably suffered as a consequence

- The helicopter back from Lukla to Kathmandu was $350 each, including transfers from the airport to our hotel

- We stayed an extra night in Thamel before and an extra night after which cost $50 per night

- We each gave the guides and porters 10% of the cost of the trip as a tip. This worked out at $140 each

- I took £1000 spending money, which covered all of the above, the cost of my painting, Caroline's perfume at Dubai airport and numerous gifts for friends and family. I could have spent significantly less, but decided to purchase bottled water, Wi-Fi, charging facilities, some extra food and drink at the teahouses and a shower when available

- I had to go for 3 courses of rabies jabs over 3 weeks at the total cost of £190 in Scotland a month before departure

- I had most of the clothing and equipment before leaving. This could prove costly if you don't have it already

- The trekking company we used was Himalayan Wonders and I would highly recommend them. Their website is himalayanwonders.com

I hope the above list and the contents of the book help you with your trip to Everest Base Camp and answer any questions you may have had.

If I have missed anything, please feel free to email me your questions to paultallett@yahoo.co.uk and I will be happy to help.

www.publishandprint.co.uk